D1462203

Truth and Lies

In Beverly Hills

By David Kennedy

Copyright © 2017 David Kennedy

ISBN-13:

978-1545014141

ISBN-10:

1545014140

1 2 3 4 5 6 7 8 9 10

Prologue

For a couple of years during the mid '90s, the Menendez Brothers, Lyle and Erik, held the country's attention as their stories played out on national television. We watched as the prosecutors described how the two boys cold-bloodedly murdered their parents for money.

Prosecutors displayed a series of graphic autopsy photos for jurors in the murder trial of Lyle and Erik Menendez that appeared to reduce the brothers from loving children to cold hearted killers.

It was in the den of their Beverly Hills mansion on North Elm Drive that Erik and Lyle gunned down their parents on August 20th, 1989.

Using 12-gauge shotguns, Lyle and Erik Menendez murdered their parents, José, an entertainment industry executive and Kitty Menendez, a former small-town beauty queen and schoolteacher.

José was shot point-blank in the back of the head. Kitty, who made a run for it, was shot multiple times.

The prosecution contended the brothers ambushed their parents, blasting them with pump-action shotguns, and then covered up the crime, beginning with shrieks and tears on their front lawn on the night of the killings. Lyle was 21 at the time; Erik was 18.

It took two trials before they were convicted.

The first, highly publicized trial was arguably one of the most controversial of the decade and ended in a mistrial. But, in the second trial, both Lyle and Erik were found guilty of first-degree murder with special circumstances and sentenced to two consecutive life sentences each, without the possibility of parole.

José and Kitty

José was born in 1944 to an upper-middle class family in Havana, Cuba. His father was a well-known soccer player who owned his own accounting firm. His mother was a swimmer who was elected to Cuba's sports hall of fame. José had two older sisters, Teresita, known as "Terry", and Marta. Although the family was not rich, José's parents' accomplishments in sports guaranteed them an honored place in Cuban society. José was

4

five years younger than Terry and was spoiled and adored by his mother.

During 1959 and 1960 Cuba was undergoing a revolution. Fulgencio Batista was overthrown and Fidel Castro came to power and made radical changes to both the economy and the social welfare system of the country. Castro's government seized the property of the upper and middle classes, turned farms into collectives and canceled all leases and mortgages. The upper and middle classes lost property, the lower classes faced higher prices and the government grew more repressive, imprisoning or executing opponents of Castro.

In 1960 José Menendez was a teenager when his parents sent him to the US from Cuba after Castro took over. José's parents saw that their lives in Cuba were forever changed. The first step they made in their decision to leave Cuba was to send their son to the United States. José flew to the United States with Terry's fiancé and settled in Hazleton, Pennsylvania, located between Scranton and Allentown.

José arrived penniless and did not speak or understand English but was determined to succeed in his adopted country. José studied diligently in high school and worked part-time to earn spending money. Due to financial hardship, José was not able to achieve one of his dreams, which was to attend an Ivy League college.

He promised himself that someday, when he had children, they would achieve his dream and graduate from an Ivy League college. Influenced by his parents, who were both champion athletes in Cuba, José also developed into a good athlete and later attended Southern Illinois University on a swimming scholarship.

José did not like Southern Illinois University and is remembered by classmates as withdrawn and sullen. José supported himself financially with his athletic scholarship, but eventually walked away from athletics to concentrate on his studies. There was one person who made José feel good. Her name was Kitty Andersen.

Kitty

Mary "Kitty" Anderson was born in 1941, the youngest of four children of Charles and Mae Andersen. Her family lived in Oak Lawn, a suburb south of Chicago. During her early childhood, Kitty's family was solidly middle class. Her father owned a heating and air-conditioning business that did well and her mother stayed at home to care for Kitty and her two older brothers, Milt and Brian, and Kitty's older sister, Joan.

Although the Andersen family appeared to be loving and close, Kitty's father beat her mother, sometimes in front of their children. Charles Andersen also beat his children. Before Kitty entered grammar school, her father left her mother for another woman.

Her mother never got over the failed marriage, and suffered from depression for the rest of her life.

In order to support her family, Kitty's mother worked for United Airlines at Midway Airport outside of Chicago. Kitty's parents eventually divorced and this was the cause of life long emotional scars for her. Throughout her childhood, Kitty was withdrawn and depressed. She had difficulty forming friendships and did not have many friends in grade or high school. Kitty's father remarried and continued to live in Oak Lawn. Her mother never remarried and became bitter and depressed by the divorce.

Kitty grew up convinced that divorce was the worst thing that could happen in a woman's life. Kitty hated her father and did not have any contact with him for many years after her parents' divorce.

In her senior year of high school, Kitty applied to and was accepted by Southern Illinois University. In 1958, her freshman year of college, Kitty began to work in the university's broadcasting department where she learned to produce dramas for radio and television. Kitty gained a great deal of confidence through her participation in these activities.

During her senior year in 1962, Kitty had enough confidence to compete in and win the Miss Oak Lawn beauty pageant sponsored by the VFW.

Kitty dreamed that after she graduated from college, she would pursue a career in producing and directing commercial radio and television programs in New York City.

Kitty and José met during Kitty's senior year and José's freshman year. After only a short time, Kitty and José became inseparable. To José, Kitty was attractive not only physically, but in what she represented. Kitty was the daughter of a shopkeeper, the offspring of the American merchant class. By winning Kitty, José was establishing his claim to his new country. José fulfilled something for Kitty too. Kitty felt that there was a depth to José that few people understood or appreciated. She saw someone who was willing to work hard and overcome hardships, not someone who was willing to slide by on family connections or money, like her privileged classmates. José told Kitty of his plan to make it big in the business world.

When José and Kitty were seen together around the Southern Illinois campus, people would stop and stare. After all it was the early 1960s, they lived in a small, conservative southern Illinois town and people from different ethnic backgrounds did not mix. The civil rights movement in America was centered in the South and had yet to reach Carbondale. Kitty was three years older than José was. Their ages and background differences did not seem to matter to Kitty and José; they were determined to spend their lives together.

José and Kitty's relationship caused problems for both of their families. Kitty's family was surprised that she would choose a Cuban teenager as her future husband. José's family thought that Kitty was beneath their social standing because her parents were divorced.

José's parents also thought that at age 19, José was too young to marry. Around the time that Kitty graduated with a Bachelor of Science degree in communications, José and Kitty eloped and were secretly married in 1963.

After their marriage, José and Kitty moved to New York City. José's parents had fled Cuba, his mother in 1961 and his father a short time later. They had settled in New York City. José gave up his athletic scholarship at Southern Illinois and transferred to Queens College, City University of New York, while Kitty found a job teaching grade school. During the early years of her marriage, Kitty's dreams of working in broadcasting began to fade and she discarded her plans to obtain a master's degree, in order to support José and his career.

Kitty's decision to sacrifice her future goals and work as a schoolteacher paid off in some ways after his career took off, but it came at a high price in terms of her emotional dependence on José.

And this dependency on José would later make her the doormat of the family.

Life after College

The Menendez family

In 1967, José graduated from Queens College with a CPA degree. He went to work for Coopers & Lybrand, an international accounting firm. Kitty continued to teach grade school.

On January 10th, 1968 the couple's first son Joséph Lyle Menendez was born in New York. José and Kitty were now more than just a couple. They were now a family.

What the world did not know at this time was that José had big plans for his new born son. And many believe that those very plans are what lead to José and Kitty's death.

In 1969, José was sent to Chicago to audit Lyon Container, a client of Coopers & Lybrand. José so impressed the management of Lyon Container that they asked him to come to work for them as the company's controller. José was twenty-five years old.

José, Kitty and their infant son, Joséph Lyle, moved to Hinsdale, Illinois. Kitty became a full time mother, while José worked hard and turned Lyon Container into a profitable company.

In 1970, José was named president of Lyon Container. The position did not last long because José and the chairman of the board became involved in a fight over the direction of the company.

In 1971, José went to work at Hertz, as an executive in the car leasing division and the Menendez family moved from Illinois back to the East Coast and settled in New Jersey.

José's second son, Erik, was born on November 27th, 1971. In 1973, José became Hertz's chief financial officer. José rose through Hertz's ranks and in 1979, when he was 35, became Hertz's worldwide general manager. At Hertz, José earned a reputation for abusing subordinates. This reputation would follow him for the remainder of his life.

Many say that José was very demanding and on many occasions he would degrade employees and it was not unlike José to yell and criticize his employees during company meeting.

In the business world José was tough. He knew what he wanted out of his employees and he did whatever it took to get what he wanted.

During his time at Hertz OJ Simpson was invited to the Menendez home for dinner.

Young Lyle and Erik were able to meet the then sports star. And in a twist of fate they would meet again on a cell block in the county jail as they all awaited trial on murder charges.

José dedicated himself to raising great sons who would carry out his plans for the future and continue his legacy. Because José had fought his way up the corporate ladder, he understood that there was an easier and more refined way to reach the top and he set about training his sons to reach that peak. When the brothers were young, José had rules for everything: what they could eat, whom they could spend time with, and what they read and thought about. Every hour of every day was to be accounted for. José and Kitty did not take in to account that they were dealing with young children, nor did they consider that their children could be flawed or that they themselves might be flawed.

Erik, left, and Lyle, right, are pictured in this undated photo together with their father José

It was during the murder trial that the boys claimed that their father started molesting them as young children.

Some people have commented on the placement of José's hand in an undated photo of him and his sons. While some say that the photo was just taken at a moment when his hand may have rested on his son's crotch area while others say that the uncomfortable look on Lyle's face and the placement of his hand on his fathers may show that the boys may have been telling the truth about the sexual abuse.

José's greatest flaw was his viciousness that probably grew out of his insecurity about his ethnicity. José relished humiliating Anglo colleagues who made mistakes, yet at the same time he sought acceptance from them through his efforts to transform himself into an American. He encouraged business colleagues to call him "Joe," rather than José.

The pressures of meeting José's demands appeared early on Lyle and Erik. Both brothers developed stutters, stomach pains and had a habit of grinding their teeth. Both brothers also developed nasty tempers.

As they grew older, the brothers were drawn to each other for companionship and solidarity in order to face their father's control. Erik grew up worshiping Lyle. Erik often told his friends how much he admired his brother. Erik's friends couldn't understand why. They thought Lyle was serious trouble. Erik's worship of Lyle probably came from the fact that José was so remote that his younger son did not feel he could approach him. Lyle was approachable, while José was an overwhelming presence.

The brothers' friends would comment that Lyle and Erik were extremely close, but that their personalities were very different. Lyle was described as aloof and witty, while Erik was described as sensitive and quiet. Lyle was also described as having the stronger personality.

Beginning when the brothers were in grade school, José posed questions about current events at the dinner table. Occasionally Erik was allowed to answer but most of the questions fell on Lyle to answer. As the brothers grew older, the questions became more complex. José decided that each brother should select one sport to excel in. José encouraged the brothers to pick a sport that did not require them to be members of a team. He felt that teamwork challenged his authority and called into question the way he was raising his sons. By the time Lyle was twelve and Erik was nine, they had selected tennis.

Later during the trial it was learned that José would wake the boys up at 4 am to practice tennis before they went to school.

In 1979, the family was living in Pennington, outside of Princeton, New Jersey. Lyle and Erik attended the Princeton Day School, a private school. At the Princeton Day School both brothers were considered average students. Lyle developed problems academically when he was in the sixth grade. His teacher found that he was not well prepared and did not have the ability to concentrate. Teachers at the Princeton Day School felt that both Lyle and Erik had learning problems, but José would not accept that his sons had flaws.

Erik grew up emulating his older brother and for a time lived in the shadow of Lyle, especially at the Princeton Day School. It seemed that neither brother fit in at school. They were both considered mysterious loners, who laughed only at their own private jokes. They did not join in or play with other children. Erik learned early in life that José was grooming Lyle to become the future leader of the family. He grew up sad and withdrawn.

Kitty and José were so adamant to portray their sons as perfect. Throughout grade and high school, Kitty completed much of the boy's homework for them. The teachers noticed that the homework the brothers turned in was far better than the work completed in class. Erik's schoolwork, like Lyle's, was average. Teachers also noticed that the brothers were immature compared to their classmates. As a young teen, Lyle still wet his bed and played with stuffed animals.

In 1980, José's career ended at Hertz. Another man was brought in and made president and José was reassigned to the entertainment division of RCA, the company that owned Hertz.

In 1981, José was assigned to RCA's record division, which was saddled with overpaid, aging recording stars. José tried to turn the division around by signing the Eurythmics and Jefferson Starship. At RCA, José's ethics came under scrutiny. An example of José's questionable ethics was his practice of shipping large quantities of albums to record stores in order to make sales appear larger than they were.

In 1986 alone, RCA was forced to honor $25 million in returned albums. By 1985, at the age of

41, José had risen to become the executive vice president and chief operating officer for RCA Records' worldwide operations. However, as hard as he tried, José was unable to turn RCA Records around.

From the beginning of their marriage, Kitty had always given José the freedom he desired. As much as he promised her that their marriage would be a partnership, in reality José made decisions for both of them, often without consulting Kitty. During his life, José acquired a number of mistresses. José's longest lasting affair began in 1978 with a woman named Louise, who was a dark-haired, self-confident businesswoman.

Louise and José traveled together and entertained as a couple in Louise's townhouse in Manhattan. José cared deeply about Louise yet never gave any thought to leaving Kitty. He also never considered ending his affair with Louise. José felt good with Louise. She buoyed his ego. For some time Kitty was not aware of José's indiscretions. José was able to sooth Kitty with false, yet convincing claims of his faithfulness, but Kitty became suspicious of his behavior.

In 1981, Kitty discovered one of José's relationships. Like her mother, Kitty grew bitter about José's infidelities and walked out of their home for several days. José managed to convince her to come home, more so for the brothers than because he loved her, according to José's brother-in-law.

There were signs that Lyle and Erik were headed for serious trouble. In 1982, when Erik and Lyle were about twelve and fifteen, their cousin Diane Vander Molen stayed with the Menendez family for the summer. One night, the three cousins began to playfully wrestle. Suddenly and without warning, Lyle and Erik began to undress Diane. Without saying a word, the brothers tied her up and stripped off her shirt.

Diane screamed and the brothers retreated from their attack. The brothers had attacked her like a pack of dogs, with no warning. As suddenly as the attack had begun, it ended. Around the same time, Diane experienced another attack. This time, she and Lyle were watching television. Without warning, Lyle struck. He climbed on top of her and began to fondle her breasts. Like the attack that came earlier, she had not enticed Lyle and the attack ceased as soon as she was able to free herself.

In 1986, at about the same time that José's career at RCA was coming to an end, Kitty found out about Louise. José told Kitty about Louise and his other affairs. This sent Kitty into a depressive spiral and she talked about committing suicide.

She became depressed and more emotionally dependent. Some believe that this was the beginning of Kitty's dependency on prescription drugs and alcohol.

Through contacts that José had made while at RCA, he was able to find a position as the President of LIVE Entertainment in California. LIVE was a video-distribution and duplication company and was partially owned by Carolco, a movie-production company, best known for producing the *Rambo* pictures. José jumped at the chance to become involved in the film business and had no problem uprooting his family and moving them from the East Coast to the West Coast.

At the time that José was brought in to run LIVE, it had posted a loss of $20 million for 1985. José saw another opportunity to turn a struggling company around. Kitty wasn't so positive about the move. She had spent the past 16 years building a life outside of her marriage.

Kitty had an established a network of friends who she cared about and who in turn cared about her. José and Kitty had recently purchased a home in Princeton, New Jersey, that Kitty considered her dream house. Nevertheless, José decided that it would be in Kitty and Erik's best interests to move to California with him.

They settled in Calabasas, an upper-middle class suburb in the northwestern part of the San Fernando Valley. Lyle remained in Princeton to attend college.

After having Lyle and Erik, Kitty had, like many mothers, gained weight. Ex-beauty-queen though she was, she now seemed to lack style in her clothing and general appearance. She lacked taste in decorating and let the housekeeping duties go. All of this worked against her in the upper middle class Los Angeles social environs she might otherwise have flourished in.

To the outside world the family presented a successful facade. But Kitty no longer trusted her husband and increasingly they were running into serious troubles with the boys.

When José, Kitty and Erik moved to California in 1986, Erik was a sophomore in high school. Erik enrolled at Calabasas High School. Away from his brother and the comparisons that were often made between them at the Princeton Day School, Erik found his own identity. Erik made friends with a group of boys who were like him, cocky, loud and with a rebellious streak.

Kitty had been worried about Erik's sexual orientation for some time. Kitty believed that Erik was homosexual. When they moved to Calabasas, Kitty gave Erik an order to find a girlfriend in six months. Erik found an older girl at Calabasas High, but their relationship was short lived. At a party, Erik and the girl argued and Erik locked the girl in a room. He would not let her leave. She screamed and yelled, but Erik would not let her out. Finally, Erik let the girl go. The girl had enough of Erik. Later she recalled that he was "one of the oddest guys I've ever met." "He's very arrogant, very confident, but deep down he's got a lot of problems and insecurities."

Erik later had another girlfriend, Janice, whom Kitty and José both liked. Unlike Lyle's girlfriends whom Kitty found cheap, Kitty thought highly of Janice. Perhaps Erik's most important relationship at Calabasas High was with Craig Cignarelli.

Craig was the captain of the tennis team and Erik was the number one-ranked player on the team. Craig and Erik spent a great deal of time together and wrote a third rate screenplay entitled *Friends*. The script was a sixty-two-page thriller about a son from a wealthy family who reads his parents' will and learns that upon their deaths, he will inherit $157 million. The son murders everyone to get his hands on his parents' money before being killed.

Lyle's first romance came when he was fifteen. His relationship with his girlfriend, Stacey Feldman, was as innocent and chaste, as the previous attacks on his cousin Diane had been perverse and sexual. Stacey managed the men's varsity tennis team at the Princeton Day School and Lyle was the number one-ranked player on the team. Their first date was to see *Raiders of the Lost Ark*. Lyle was a huge movie fan and going to the movies was, perhaps, the only experience that Lyle was able to enjoy for himself without having it filtered through his parents.

Lyle seemed to have grown up completely believing to be true what he saw on the movie screen. He never seemed to be able to distinguish between fact and fiction.

Stacey and Lyle fell in love. They walked around Princeton Day hand in hand which was against the rules. Teachers and administrators let this infraction pass because they felt that Stacey and Lyle were awkward kids who needed each other. At the end of the school year, Lyle and Stacey were voted "most married" by their classmates.

Lyle and Stacey talked about getting married and having children. Lyle lavished jewelry and other gifts on Stacey. Stacey ended the relationship when she went off to college, realizing that she wanted to experience more of life and that she was too young to get married. Lyle was hurt by Stacey's rejection and tried to win her back by promising to buy her a fur coat. Stacey was not interested and Lyle moved on.

José dreamed that Lyle would attend an Ivy League college. Lyle, who was not a good student, told his friends that he wanted to skip college and open a restaurant with his father's financial backing. José would not entertain thoughts of anything less than an Ivy League education for Lyle.

It was also later revealed that Lyle started to lose his hair in 1985. José went to the extreme to purchase a toupee for his son to wear so that people would not notice the hair loss. José told him that it was better for his image if it appeared that he had a full head of hair.

When Lyle initially applied to Princeton in 1986, he was rejected. He enrolled in a local community college and submitted another application to Princeton for the 1987 school year. While Lyle waited to hear from Princeton, he met and began to date Jaime Pisarcik, a waitress at a local Princeton restaurant. Jaime was also a tennis player and five years older than Lyle was. Kitty and José did not like Jaime because they felt that Jaime was dating Lyle because he was the son of wealthy parents.

Lyle was accepted to Princeton in 1987, more on the strength of his ethnicity and ability to play tennis, than on his standardized test scores and high school grades that were just average. During the summer of 1987, Lyle and Jaime announced that they were engaged. This announcement angered José.

At 19, José felt that Lyle was too young to be married. Shortly before Lyle was to begin at Princeton, Jaime moved to Alabama to teach tennis. Lyle followed her. José was upset by this and secretly arranged to sponsor Jaime on a European tennis tour. José thought that once Jaime was out of the picture, Lyle could concentrate on Princeton without any distractions. José was wrong. Lyle followed Jaime to Europe.

Final admission to Princeton is contingent on each admitted freshman signing a letter promising to obey the honor code. The honor code has been in place at Princeton since 1893. Lyle signed it probably thinking that any trouble he got himself into could be handled using the ways José had taught him: lie, cheat, steal, but don't get caught.

During his first semester at Princeton, Lyle was accused of plagiarism. Specifically, Lyle was required to complete a laboratory assignment in his Psychology 101 class, a freshman level course. Lyle was accused of copying a lab partner's homework assignment and turning the assignment in as his own work. When Lyle realized how much trouble he was in; he asked Brendan Scott, a priest and doctoral student, to assist him with his defense. Lyle told Brendan that he had missed a number of previous assignments in class and, because of this, could not afford to miss another. During this time, Lyle was traveling back and forth on weekends to California to visit his family. During the weekend before this psychology lab was due, Lyle had traveled to California and lost his notebook with his notes in the airport. Lyle asked his lab partner if he could look at his assignment. The assignment that Lyle handed in resembled Lyle's lab partner's work so closely that the instructor singled it out and brought it to the attention of campus authorities.

José found out about the plagiarism accusation from his sister, Terry, in whom Lyle had confided. At first, José did not think there would be any serious consequences for Lyle. José sent Lyle a statement to read about ethics before the disciplinary committee. Lyle, as usual, when he was in trouble, tried to cover himself in José's protective cloak. Both José and Lyle underestimated the trouble that Lyle was in. After a four-hour hearing, the disciplinary committee deliberated for one hour and found Lyle guilty of plagiarism and suspended him for one year. After learning of the outcome, José flew immediately to Princeton for a meeting with Princeton's president.

At the meeting, José argued that the punishment was unduly harsh and did not fit the crime. José argued that this was just one homework assignment and not a large part of Lyle's grade for the class. The president was unmoved and informed Lyle that he could return to Princeton in 1988 in good standing.

Lyle had come face to face with the heart of Princeton and failed Princeton's test. Lyle hated school and rarely participated in campus activities. He was so devoted to winning and being first that he had a difficult time just being one of many struggling students competing at an Ivy League college. Although Lyle was humiliated and wanted to transfer to UCLA, or the University of Pennsylvania, José would not hear of it.

In July 1988, Erik and Lyle began breaking into homes in Calabasas. The brothers burglarized the homes owned by parents of their friends and were surprised by the large amounts of cash and jewelry that they were able to steal. The brothers had found an easy source of spending money, rather than having to ask José for a hand out, or listen to José lecture about hard work.

The amount of money and jewelry that Lyle and Erik stole was estimated to be more than $100,000, large enough to be classified as a felony offense called grand theft burglary. The Los Angeles County sheriff's detective who investigated the burglaries received a break in the case after Erik was stopped for a driving violation in Calabasas and stolen property was found in his car trunk. Later the detective discovered that a safe in one of the homes that the brothers had burglarized was found in another home burglarized by the brothers. It appeared that the thieves had developed a guilty conscience and returned a safe they had stolen to the wrong home.

José was furious about the burglaries. José did not want his sons to spend any time in jail and hired Gerald Chaleff, a well-respected criminal defense attorney to represent them. Chaleff was able to work out an agreement with the Los Angeles County district attorney's office that would absolve Lyle of any participation in the burglaries, if Erik took responsibility for all the crimes. Erik was a juvenile and had no previous record. Chaleff was able to convince a judge to sentence Erik to community service with the homeless and for the brothers to undergo psychological counseling. José wrote a check for $11,000 to the victims to cover the stolen items. The brothers had already disposed of the items and could not return them.

The burglaries were the talk of Calabasas. It seemed that neighbors of the Menendez family were uncomfortable knowing that Lyle and Erik were free and not the least bit remorseful. José blamed Erik's friends, instead of Erik for the burglaries, just as he had blamed Princeton for Lyle's plagiarism rather than Lyle. José probably had a difficult time understanding the brothers' behavior and why Lyle and Erik had victimized friends, people they supposedly valued.

During the year that Lyle was out of school, José made sure that he was kept busy. José was concerned that he was giving his sons too many advantages and creating rich spoiled brats. José put Lyle to work at LIVE. Lyle was responsible for reviewing expense reports and looking for ways to improve efficiency and reduce costs. Lyle was treated like any other employee and had to make an appointment to see José.

Even though Lyle's employment at LIVE was brief, it left a deep and lasting impression on him. Lyle saw how the atmosphere in the office grew tense when José was around and how José berated employees in front of other employees. Lyle told his friends that he was resented at LIVE because he was the boss's son. The fact was that Lyle was resented at LIVE, not because he was the boss's son, but because of his lack of effort.

Lyle was remembered by those at LIVE as showing up late and unapologetic for work, ignoring orders, not paying attention and skipping work entirely on warm days to play tennis. "Nasty, arrogant, and self-centered," was the way some co-workers described Lyle. Finally one of José's associates went to him and complained about Lyle. José asked the associate what he would do if Lyle was not the boss's son and the associate said fire him, so Lyle was fired.

José began to complain about living in Calabasas. He told people at LIVE that the family was receiving harassing telephone calls and that his tires had been slashed. It may have all been talk and a way of José saving face rather than admitting that he was embarrassed of the boys and the fact that they robbed their own neighbors.

He told associates that he felt that he and his family would be safer living in Beverly Hills.

These were not the only burglaries that the police were able to pin on the Menendez brothers. In April 1988, two burglaries took place at the New Jersey office of the Sierra Club and the office of the Princeton Friends of Open Spaces. In these burglaries, office equipment was stolen with a value of approximately $1,100.

The offices were housed in the same property that the Menendez family owned just before they moved to California and the house in which Lyle had lived in before entering Princeton. José and Kitty had sold the house in November 1987. The police were left with few clues as to who committed the burglaries. In both burglaries, the burglar had entered the home through a second floor bathroom.

The police were finally able to connect Lyle to the burglaries after a confidential police informant came forward. The informant told the police that one day during the summer of 1988; he had been riding to the beach with the Menendez brothers when Lyle played a cassette tape. The tape was a recording of voices talking. There was also background noise. Lyle bragged to the police informant that they were listening to a tape recording of a burglary that Lyle committed at his old house in Princeton.

Lyle was never charged with these burglaries. By the time the police were able to connect Lyle to these crimes, he was already in jail on more serious charges.

When Lyle returned to Princeton in the fall of 1988, he continued his relationship with Jaime Pisarcik. Lyle's return to Princeton began badly when he discovered that he was assigned a roommate. Lyle wanted a single. According to the hall's student advisor, when Lyle saw the belongings of the other student in the room, he threw them in the hall. The student advisor said that Lyle had an *"I'll do what I want, when I want to"* attitude.

When Lyle told his father of his college living situation José came to Lyle's defense. He wrote a letter to Princeton requesting a single for Lyle. Lyle was given a single and like the previous year, did not participate in any campus activities. The only outside activity that Lyle seemed to show any interest in was cultivating friendships with a group of students who were also jocks.

In February 1989, Jaime introduced Lyle to Donovan Goodreau. Donovan came to Princeton after spending two years at a junior college in Northern California. He had always wanted to travel and made his way across the country, winding up in Princeton because he was attracted to the school's reputation and the large number of people his own age. Donovan was trying to sort out his future plans.

Lyle and Donovan found they had a lot in common and Donovan soon became Lyle's best friend. Goodreau eventually moved into Lyle's room at Princeton, which was against the rules since he was not a student at the university. But then, Lyle had once kept a puppy in his room at Princeton, and having animals in the rooms was against the rules, too.

Kitty and José were glad to have Donovan around because now that they were living in California, they could no longer complete Lyle's homework for him. Donovan was willing to write Lyle's papers for him, in an effort to keep Lyle from failing.

During the spring of 1989, Lyle began to date a model named Christy. Christy was 30 years old, nine years older than Lyle was. This relationship upset both José and Kitty. There was another issue that upset José even more and that was Lyle's continued desire to transfer to UCLA. Lyle was tired of Princeton, but José would not entertain any thoughts of Lyle transferring to another school.

After Lyle returned from spring break, Donovan was accused of stealing from students in Lyle's dorm. Rather than defend Donovan, who insisted he was innocent of the thefts, Lyle confronted him with two of his friends. Donovan was forced to leave Princeton.

In his haste to leave Lyle's dorm room, Donovan forgot to pack his wallet that contained his driver's license, Social Security card and other identification.

That same fall, those contents that Donavan accidently left behind will play a crucial part in one of America's most famous murders.

August 1989

On August 18th, just two days before the murders someone entered a Big 5 sporting-goods store in San Diego and purchased two Mossberg twelve-gauge shotguns in, using the driver's license of Donovan Goodreau.

Under federal law, to purchase a weapon, an individual must fill out a 4473 form, which requires the buyer to provide his name, address, and signature, as well as an identification card with picture. Donovan Goodreau has subsequently said on television that he can prove he was in New York City at the time of purchase, that the signature did not even resemble his own and that the address given was false.

The investigation team would later discover this link between the Menendez brothers and two Mossberg 12-gauge shotguns.

Not only was Lyle underachieving academically at Princeton University, Lyle's 'I'll do whatever I like' attitude had him put on disciplinary probation for damaging pool tables in his hall of residence. He also had his driver's license suspended and lost the family's privileges at their country club in Princeton.

Exasperated with their sons' behavior, José and Kitty threatened to cut out the boys from their wills.

Kitty, who was undergoing psychiatric counselling, told her therapist on July 19th, 1989, a month before she was murdered, that her sons were *"narcissistic, lacked conscience and exhibited signs that they were sociopaths"*.

In an effort to share some time together as a family and perhaps lessen some of the tension that everyone had been feeling, José and Kitty chartered a boat to go shark fishing with the boys.

On Saturday August 19th, a day before the murders, the Menendez family travelled to Marina del Ray, the largest man-made small boat harbor in the world, four miles from Los Angeles International Airport.

The boat's crew later reported that the Menendez family seemed miserable and non-communicative, with José fishing from the back of the boat, the brothers keeping to themselves at the front of the boat, and Kitty below deck due to seasickness.

The following is an account of the events surrounding the murder of José and Kitty Menendez, as pieced together by police investigators and medical examiners. Years later, at trial, Lyle and Erik would paint a very different picture.

Menendez home at 722 Elm Drive in L.A.

On the evening of Sunday August 20th, 1989, José and Kitty were relaxing in the family room of their extensive Beverly Hills mansion, 722 Elm Drive, eating dessert and dozing while a James Bond thriller, The Spy Who Loved Me, played on the VCR. Their sons were out for the evening.

It was warm in Beverly Hills that evening. The maid had the night off and the white, $4 million,

40

23-room Mediterranean-style mansion at 722 Elm Drive was quiet.

Around 10:00 p.m., a teenage girl was outside her home, located down the street from the Menendez mansion, waiting for her boyfriend. The girl noticed a small car drive up and stop in front of the Menendez home. There were two men inside the car. The men exited from the car. One man went to the trunk and the other walked toward the house. The girl lost interest and looked away.

The Menendez mansion was set back from the street, shaded by dense foliage and protected by an elaborate security system. The house had previously been rented to a succession of business and entertainment people, including the artist formerly known as Prince and Elton John.

A high iron fence surrounded the mansion and there were iron gates barring the entrance to the semicircular driveway in front of the home. On this evening, the gates located in front of the driveway were open and the security system was off.

The men entered the home through the French doors in the study. They walked down the hallway toward the family room, located in the back of the house. The men entered the family room, which was illuminated only by the light coming from the television screen.

José was dozing on the tan leather couch, sitting at the end nearest the door leading to the hallway. José's legs were stretched out in front of him; his feet were on the coffee table along with two dishes that contained the remains of a berry and ice cream snack. Kitty was lying under a blanket, her body stretched out across the couch, her head in José's lap.

One of the men pointed his twelve-gauge Mossberg shotgun loaded with ball-bearing sized pellets, at José and squeezed the trigger. Two shots were fired; one shattered the glass and splintered the wood of the French doors behind the couch where José was sitting. One pellet struck José in the left elbow; another struck him in the right arm, followed by another.

The shots immobilized José. One of the killers walked behind José and placed the shotgun against the back of his head and fired. The second was a contact shot to the back of his head that blew open his skull and killed him.

José's lifeless body came to rest on the couch, slumped slightly to the right. His hands rested on his stomach and his feet on the floor.

After the first shots were fired at José, Kitty became alert. She woke up to find herself spattered by José's blood and body tissue. Kitty stood and began to turn away from her attackers, taking a step or two before being shot in the right leg near her calf and in her right arm. Kitty fell between the couch and the coffee table. She struggled to stand again and tried to regain her balance, but she slipped as she stepped into her own blood. She stood long enough for her blood to flow vertically down her leg. She tried desperately to walk away, but another shot was fired, which brought her down. Now that she was on the floor, her killers fired indiscriminately, riddling her body with shotgun pellets. Kitty was hit in the left thigh from a range that was so close that the paper wadding that contained the pellets caused her leg to break. She was shot in the right arm, then the left breast, which perforated her left lung. A quart of her blood flowed into her chest cavity. Kitty was not dead. She continued to breathe and tried to crawl away from where she was felled, but could not.

The killers were out of ammunition. They paused, unsure of what to do next. They probably wondered if Kitty would be able to identify them and tell the police who they were and what had happened. They decided they could not take a chance on this happening and ran to the car to get more ammunition.

They reloaded their shotguns with birdshot, instead of the ball-bearing sized pellets that they had used before.

One of the killers ran back inside the house and into the family room where Kitty lay dying. The killer leaned over the coffee table and placed the shotgun against Kitty's left cheek and fired. She had been shot four times in her head and ten times in her body, including a shot that had almost severed her right thumb.

The killer was not finished. He shot both José and Kitty near the left knee. The final act the killers performed was to carefully gather the shell casings from the spreading pools of blood that now covered the couch, floor and rug under the coffee table.

The 9-1-1 Call

Following the movie, Lyle and Erik drove to Santa Monica but apparently got lost and missed their friend. They called Berman from a public telephone and made further plans to meet him at the Cheesecake Factory restaurant in Beverly Hills.

They then drove home allegedly to collect Erik's fake ID so that he could buy alcohol when they were at the restaurant. It was then that they discovered their parents had been killed and called 9-1-1.

At 11:47 p.m. a 9-1-1 call was received at the Beverly Hills Police Department.

This was about an hour and a half after the neighbor girl said that she seen the two men in the driveway.

The department runs a tape recorder continuously in order to record every call received by the 9-1-1 emergency department.

Dispatcher: Beverly Hills emergency.

Lyle Menendez: Yes, police, uh...

Dispatcher: What's the problem?

Lyle: We're the sons (caller begins to sob)...

Dispatcher: What's the problem? What's the problem?

Lyle: (Still crying) They shot and killed my parents!

Dispatcher: What? Who? Are they still there?

Lyle: Yes.

Dispatcher: The people who...

Lyle: No, no.

Dispatcher: They were shot?

Lyle: Erik, man, don't.

Dispatcher: (Talking over the background sounds of screams and Lyle shouting, "Erik, shut up!") I have a hysterical person on the phone. Is the person still there?

Second Dispatcher: What happened? Have you been able to figure out what happened?

Lyle: I don't know.

Second Dispatcher: You came home and found who shot?

Lyle: My mom and dad.

First Dispatcher: Are they still in the house, the people who did the shooting?

Lyle: (Screaming) Erik! Get away from them!

Second Dispatcher: Who is the person who is shot?

Lyle: My mom and dad!

The call was only two and one-half minutes in length. A minute or so later, Michael Butkus, a Beverly Hills police officer, and his partner, John Czarnocki, arrived at 722 Elm Drive. After walking around the outside of the mansion for several minutes the police officers heard screaming and watched as two men ran out of the front door, side by side, almost in step. The men ran past the officers and through the gate in front of the driveway and fell to their knees on the grass between the sidewalk and street.

Over and over again they shouted, "Oh my God, I can't believe it!"

The two cops tried to get information out of the men, but the younger one was irrational, running around and trying to ram his head into a tree. The older one was trying to restrain and calm the younger one.

In their attempts to draw suspicion away from themselves, the brothers told the police some strange things. They said that upon their arrival home, before discovering their parents' bodies, they noticed smoke in the house and in particular in the family room.

Neither Butkus nor Czarnocki, the officers who arrived at the scene minutes after Lyle had placed the 9-1-1 call, had noticed any smoke.

Lyle also told police that his mother had been suicidal for the past few years and had been edgy and behaving oddly, and Erik suggested possible Mafia involvement in his parents' deaths.

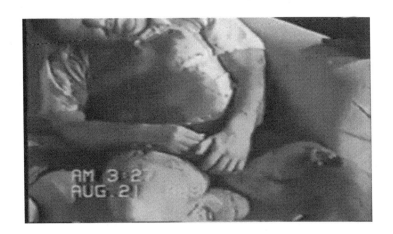

Shortly after Butkus and Czarnocki discovered the bodies of José and Kitty Menendez, Detective Les Zoeller received a call at home from Marvin Iannone, the Chief of the Beverly Hills Police Department, informing him that he was being appointed to head the investigation of the Menendez murders. Zoeller was 38, but looked younger and was considered to be the Beverly Hills Police Department's top investigator.

Until the Menendez murders, Zoeller's most challenging case had been the "Billionaire Boys Club" (BBC) investigation. The BBC was an investment fraternity and social club dreamed up by Joe Hunt. The BBC was set up to bring its members, young men from affluent backgrounds, wealth through stock and commodity market speculation. The BBC failed, but not before ringing up $900,000 in losses and spawning at least two murders. Zoeller made the case against Joe Hunt, who was convicted of murder and sentenced to life in prison without parole.

A second BBC member, Reza Eslaminia, was convicted of murdering his father and also sentenced to life in prison.

When Zoeller arrived at the Elm Drive mansion, he noticed that nothing had been stolen from the mansion. Although the family room where the murders were committed was messy, it appeared that the clutter was not the result of a room that had been turned upside in a robbery. It appeared as though the victims were acquainted with their killers and Zoeller noticed that there was no forced entry into the home.

Lyle and Erik were taken to the police department for questioning. The police did not consider them suspects and wanted to see if the brothers knew anything about the crime. Sergeant Thomas Edmonds, the police detective supervisor, questioned the brothers. During the questioning, Erik became distraught. He began to sob and was unable to sit still. Lyle was under control and answered questions methodically. After twenty minutes, the questioning ceased because Erik broke down uncontrollably.

The brothers provided the police with a chronology of how they spent August 20, 1989.

They described how they had played tennis in the morning on the tennis court behind the house, watched part of a tennis match on television and spent the afternoon shopping at the Beverly Center, a local shopping mall. Around 5:00 p.m. they made plans to get together with a friend at "Taste of LA," a local food festival in Santa Monica. The brothers said they left home around 8:00 p.m., to go to Westwood Village to see *License to Kill*, the new James Bond film, but the lines were too long, so they went to the Century City mall to see *Batman*. After *Batman*, the brothers drove to Santa Monica, but got lost on the way and missed their friend. From a pay phone, the brothers called their friend, Perry Berman. Berman and the brothers made plans to meet at the Cheesecake Factory in Beverly Hills. After they called Berman, the brothers drove home to get Erik's fake ID so Erik could buy alcoholic drinks.

The brothers told the police that when they returned home, they noticed smoke in the house, especially in the family room. This seemed odd to Zoeller because Butkus and Czarnocki had not seen anything like that. Lyle told Edmonds about his mother's nervous mood and her locking doors. Lyle said that his mother was on the verge of contemplating suicide and that she "was very edgy and suicidal in the last few years." Lyle didn't explain that Kitty had emotional problems for many years and that she had made a half-hearted suicide attempt two years earlier using prescription drugs. Edmonds asked Lyle who hated his parents enough to want to kill them. Edmonds was surprised when Lyle answered "maybe the mob."

Because the brothers were not suspected of killing their parents, the police did not administer gunshot-residue tests. These tests can determine whether a person has recently fired a weapon. In Beverly Hills, detectives are trained to perform these tests by the Los Angeles County Sheriff's department. It is left up to the discretion of the Beverly Hills detective assigned to a particular case to determine whether to administer the test or not.

Three days after José and Kitty Menendez were murdered; Dr. Irwin Golden of the Los Angeles County Coroner's office conducted their autopsies.

José's autopsy took place first. The first wound that Dr. Golden examined was the shotgun wound to José's head. Golden described the wound as a "gaping laceration," that was five inches by four inches, large enough for an adult to thrust his fist through the wound. The brain had been pulverized. There was also a "deformity of the face" caused by multiple fractures of the facial and jawbones. Soot was also found in the wound, indicating that when the fatal shot was fired, the gun had literally been placed against the back of José's head.

The remainder of José's wounds would not have been immediately fatal, although all resulted in much loss of blood. There were two shots to the right arm, one below the shoulder that fractured the humerus and the other to the right forearm. There was a shot to the left elbow. The trajectory of the shot was from back to front, indicating that this shot could have been one of the first shots fired at José as the killer walked around to the front of the couch to face him. José was shot in the lower left knee, creating a three-inch wound that fractured left femur. Golden discovered that there was bleeding into José's body tissues along all of the wound paths. This meant that José's heart had been pumping blood and that the wound at the back of his head, which investigators initially thought was the first shot fired at José, was not. Golden said he could not determine the order of the shots fired at José.

Kitty's autopsy revealed that she had been shot in the left cheek which caused a one-inch hole in her face that had fractured her upper jaw and dislodged four of her upper teeth. There were additional wounds to Kitty's skull, fractures to her lower jaw, and pellet wounds to her tongue. A shot had also lacerated her brain. Dr. Golden found birdshot in Kitty's wounds which confirmed the investigator's suspicions that Kitty's killers had reloaded their weapons.

None of José's wounds contained birdshot. Kitty had three wounds to her face. The most damaging was four inches and extended from Kitty's right cheek across her nose to her left cheek. Golden also discovered that Kitty's right thumb was almost severed. Investigators theorized that Kitty had extended her hand to block the shotgun blast that caused the four-inch wound in her face as a last effort at self-preservation.

The only problem with this theory was that the wound to Kitty's hand was on the palm side, not the back of her hand. Most people extend their hands palms out when attempting to defend themselves. Kitty's wound indicated she extended either her blocking hand in a strange position, or she did not want to see who was shooting at her.

Kitty also had shotgun wounds to her right forearm and left breast and three wounds to her left leg. The final wound was to her left knee. The shot was from front to back and that was odd because it came from a different angle than the other shots fired at her leg. Investigators theorized that this might have been the last shot fired at Kitty and an attempt to make the murder appear to be a mob hit.

Lives of Luxury

The graves in Princeton Cemetery

Lyle and Erik staged an elaborate memorial service for José and Kitty on August 25, 1989 at the Directors Guild of America in Los Angeles. Lyle and Erik arrived one hour late. Erik looked uncomfortable, and his face was red and swollen. Lyle appeared calm and cool. To Lyle, this event marked his arrival in the business world.

Up to this moment, the world had known Lyle through José's bragging of his accomplishments on the tennis court and his admission to Princeton. Lyle wanted to prove that he was ready to take his place as the head of the Menendez family and he was determined to assert himself as José's legitimate replacement.

At the funeral Lyle wore his father's shoes as a symbol of filling his father's shoes in life.

On August 28th, a traditional church service was held at the university chapel in Princeton. Brendan Scott conducted the service.

Scott was the faculty fellow who two years earlier had unsuccessfully assisted Lyle when he was charged with plagiarism.

At the service, Lyle spoke for thirty minutes and recalled how much José and Kitty had meant to him. Erik was too upset to speak.

Their parents' murders affected Lyle and Erik differently. Erik was unsure whether to begin attending UCLA or devote himself to tennis. Lyle seemed more focused. He decided against continuing with his college education and began to plan for a career in business.

Four days after the murders, the brothers began a spending spree. The brothers' shopping sprees were funded by José's personal life insurance policy of $650,000. The brothers spent money on new cars, designer label clothes and jewelry. Three days after the murders, the brothers spent $15,000 on Rolex watches and money clips.

The bulk of the estate's assets were a house on fourteen acres in Calabasas that José and Kitty had purchased, but never lived in, and the Beverly Hills mansion. When the loans on both properties were deducted, the value of José's real estate was $5.7 million. At the time of his death, José owned 330,000 shares of LIVE Entertainment that had been trading around at $20 per share. Added to all of this were José and Kitty's personal property and automobiles. The estate José and Kitty left was valued at $14 million, Lyle and Erik would each inherit about $2 million after loans and taxes were subtracted.

$2 million is not a small inheritance, but it fell far short of Lyle and Erik's expectations. A friend of Erik's said that the brothers had expected to inherit $90 million. The brothers were convinced that José had hidden $75 million in a secret Swiss bank account. Neither brother could explain how José could have amassed that type of fortune. According to Erik's friend, it just seemed reasonable to Lyle and Erik that José would have accumulated far more than $14 million.

About a week after the murders, Lyle and Erik met with executives at LIVE Entertainment to discuss any assets the brothers might receive from the company. The brothers were surprised to learn that the $5 million "key man" life insurance policy that LIVE had purchased for José was not valid because José had failed to take the physical examination required by the insurance company. The $15 million "key man" policy that LIVE held in the event of José's death was in effect and would give the company its most profitable quarter since the company's inception.

The brothers decided that they could not stay in the Beverly Hills mansion. The brothers told their friends that they moved from hotel to hotel because they feared that the same mobsters who murdered their parents would come after them. Immediately after the murders, LIVE paid an $8,800 bill at the Bel Air Hotel that the brothers ran up. $2,000 of the bill was for room service for the five-day stay. LIVE also paid for limousine rides and bodyguards for the brothers.

After living at various luxury hotels in Beverly Hills, the brothers rented adjoining apartments in the Marina City Towers in Marina del Rey. Lyle's apartment rented for $2,150 per month and Erik's apartment rented for $2,450 per month. The brothers saw a penthouse in one of the towers that they liked for $990,000 and put a down payment on it, but the financing fell through and they were unable to purchase it.

Lyle hired bodyguards to travel with him for several weeks after the murders. Lyle's bodyguards were alarmed when Lyle would jump out of the limousine before it came to a complete stop to shop and spend money. On one occasion, the bodyguards watched as he purchased $24,000 in stereo equipment. On September 4, Lyle told the bodyguards he no longer needed their services because his uncle had contacted someone in the mob and arranged some type of deal. Lyle didn't explain how his uncle, a middle-aged business man from a New Jersey suburb, would go about contacting the mob, or how his uncle managed to remove a sentence of death from his nephews' heads.

The brothers' shopping sprees continued. Lyle decided that he had to have a new car. The red Alfa Romeo that his parents had purchased for him as a high school graduation present and that he never liked had to go. The Alfa was replaced by a much more expensive gunmetal gray Porsche 911 Carrera that cost $64,000. Erik traded in his Ford Escort for a Jeep Wrangler.

By October 1989, Lyle had charged more than $90,000 to José's American Express card. He would travel frequently between New Jersey and California on the MGM Grand, an airline that catered to business people with expense accounts, while he was busy trying to establish Menendez Investment Enterprises.

Lyle gathered his friends from Princeton together and made them officers of Menendez Investment

Enterprises. He rented an office for $3,000 a month in a Princeton shopping mall and furnished it with expensive furniture. Menendez Investment Enterprises never moved into the suite. The office sat unused and served as a testament to Lyle's ability to create the proper setting. The friends that Lyle asked to join him were Princeton athletes, some of whom, like Lyle, had run into trouble with campus authorities. It was not difficult to see why Menendez Investment Enterprises never got off the ground; all the members were young, inexperienced in business and strangely had only known Lyle for several months. None of the members had any business skills. It seemed as if Lyle played at running a business. He dressed and acted the part, but there was little, if any substance, to anything Lyle did.

Lyle's longtime dream was to own a restaurant. He tried to buy Teresa's Pizza; a takeout pizzeria located across from Princeton's front gate but Lyle offended the co-owner and he wouldn't sell. Lyle decided to buy Chuck's Spring Street Cafe, a snack shop in Princeton that specialized in spicy chicken wings. Lyle paid $550,000 for Chuck's which the co-owner of Teresa's Pizza thought was "ridiculous" because it was only worth about

"$200,000." Many people thought Lyle was in over his head, but his uncles authorized the sale and took out a loan against the estate to finance the deal. Lyle's uncles hoped that the restaurant would bring some focus to Lyle's chaotic life. Lyle immediately went to work on Chuck's. He expanded the home delivery hours from 12:00 p.m. to 1:00 a.m. and changed the name of the restaurant to Mr. Buffalo's. Merchants in Princeton thought this was crazy since Chuck's had name recognition that was built up over many years.

After purchasing Chuck's, Lyle announced he wanted to open a second location in a nearby Princeton mall. He was also thinking of opening locations near UCLA and another in New Brunswick, New Jersey, near Rutgers University. Eventually, he wanted to open a new Mr. Buffalo's every two months. Lyle was way ahead of himself. Chuck's/Mr. Buffalo's was losing money because Lyle allowed his friends to freeload off of him.

Erik also was taken advantage of when he tried to sponsor a rock concert at the Palladium in Los Angeles. Erik gave $40,000 to a partner as his half of the payment needed for the concert. The partner disappeared along with Erik's money. Erik decided he wasn't cut out for the business world or for college and would try the professional tennis tour. He hired a private tennis coach for $60,000 a year. Erik and the coach began to travel extensively, staying at expensive hotels and spending whatever Erik thought he needed to sharpen his game.

The Investigation

Detective Les Zoeller and his partner, Detective Tim Linehan, had the difficult job of trying to solve the Menendez murders. They were confronted with many suspects and a number of theories about who may have committed the murders. José had his share of enemies and the detectives were hearing horror stories about José's behavior from almost everyone that they interviewed.

Zoeller interviewed José and Kitty's friends from Calabasas, Peter and Karen Wiere. Zoeller asked Peter Wiere what his first impression of the case was and Wiere said, "I have no basis for this, but I wonder if the boys did it." Zoeller was surprised at this. He asked Wiere to elaborate and Wiere said that Lyle and Erik always seemed to be too good to be true. The brothers seemed too polite, too deferential to adults and to Wiere, something seemed to be off.

Zoeller and the rest of the Beverly Hills investigators watched as the brothers threw money around. Kitty and José were murdered on August 20, 1989 and by the end of the year, Lyle and Erik had spent more than a million dollars. The police now suspected that the brothers were behind the murders.

Computer expert Glen Stevens

Besides the spending sprees, the police were suspicious of the brothers because they had called a computer expert on August 31, 1989 to erase the files in Kitty's computer. The police learned about Kitty's computer from Glen Stevens, a friend of Lyle's. Glen told the police that Lyle had told him that he erased the new will and called a computer expert to ensure that no one would be able to retrieve the computer file.

On October 24, Les Zoeller interviewed Erik Menendez at the Beverly Hills mansion. He told

Erik that he had heard that the brothers were not getting along. Erik complained that Lyle was spending too much money. Erik also complained that Lyle was "being just like my father." Glen Stevens told Zoeller that Lyle was "trying to manipulate his brother" and get Erik's half of the money.

Although Erik appeared cool and calm to Zoeller during the interview, Erik was shaken to his core. As soon as the interview was concluded, Erik called Lyle in Princeton. He couldn't reach him. He needed someone to talk to and confide in, so he called his psychotherapist, Jerome Oziel.

Confessing to Murder

In another, less fashionable area of the city known as Carthay Circle, an attractive thirty-seven-year-old woman named Judalon Rose Smyth, pronounced Smith, was living out her own drama in a complicated love affair with a married man who she says had told her he was divorcing his wife. Judalon Smyth's lover was a Beverly Hills psychologist named Jerome Oziel, whom she called Jerry.

Dr. Oziel was the same Dr. Oziel whom Kitty Menendez's psychologist, Les Summerfield, had recommended to her a year earlier as the doctor for her troubled son, after the judge in the burglary case in Calabasas had ruled that Erik must have counseling while he was on probation. During that brief period of court-ordered therapy, Jerome Oziel had met the entire Menendez family.

Judalon Smyth, however, was as unknown to Lyle and Erik as they were to her, and yet, seven months from the time of the double murder, she would be responsible for their arrest on the charge of killing their parents.

Erik went to see Oziel on October 31. During the session, Oziel and Erik walked around Beverly Hills. Oziel encouraged Erik to talk about his depression and suicidal thoughts. A short time later, Oziel and Erik walked back to Oziel's office. As they neared the office, Erik stopped walking and leaned against a parking meter. Oziel stopped walking as well and Erik said, "We did it. We killed our parents."

Erik told Oziel about the "Billionaire Boys Club" miniseries and how he and Lyle had watched it together. After the miniseries was shown, they talked about their shared belief that José was planning to disinherit them from his will and how terrible their lives were because José dominated them. Spurred on by the miniseries, the brothers told each other that they should kill José. Kitty presented a problem because the brothers did not want to kill her, but could not think of a way to kill their father without murdering her. At this point Oziel stopped Erik from saying anything more and had him call Lyle. Lyle raced over to Oziel's office. Before Lyle arrived at Oziel's office, Erik continued telling his story. He told Oziel about a trip to San Diego to purchase shotguns and how the brothers thought that they had committed the perfect crime. They had been careful and cleaned up the shotgun casings. They did not have to worry about fingerprints because the crime was committed in their own home so naturally their fingerprints would be everywhere. Once they had finished cleaning up, Lyle drove Erik's car to Mulholland Drive, a winding road that runs from the Pacific Ocean to the San Fernando Valley. Erik was too shaken to drive so he gave directions to Lyle as he drove. They stopped on Mulholland Drive and Erik waited until the area was cleared of cars and then threw the shotguns into a nearby canyon. They headed for a gas station where they dumped their blood-spattered clothing and shoes into a dumpster along with the shell casings. Then they drove home. They had intended to drive to the Cheesecake Factory to meet up with their friend Perry, but Erik was falling apart, so they went home and called the police.

Lyle was furious when he arrived at Oziel's office. He was angry that Erik had told Oziel everything. Lyle told Oziel that he thought José would be proud of him for committing such an effective murder. Oziel explained to the brothers the difference between a crime that takes place in a moment of heated passion, such as during an argument, and a crime committed to reach a specific goal. Oziel explained that the behavior in the latter situation was considered the behavior of a sociopath. Oziel would later testify in court that the brothers "looked at each other and said, 'We're sociopaths.'" Lyle then erupted in anger. He threatened Oziel and told Oziel that if he told anyone he would kill him too.

On November 2, the brothers met with Oziel again. Lyle threatened Oziel again, telling him that he and Erik had considered killing him in order to keep their secret. Oziel could have reported Lyle and Erik to the police because they had threatened him and this threat erased the patient-therapist confidentiality barrier, but he did not. Instead, he made notes and tape recordings of his sessions with the brothers.

On November 17, Zoeller and Linehan interviewed Erik's friend Craig Cignarelli. Cignarelli told the detectives that shortly after the murders had occurred, he had visited Erik at the Beverly Hills mansion. Erik had asked Craig if he wanted to know how it happened. Craig knew immediately what "it" was. Erik told Craig that on the night of the murders, he and Lyle had come home to get his fake ID. As Erik was walking toward his car, after finding his ID, Lyle met him with their shotguns. "Let's do it," Lyle said. According to Craig, the plan was that Lyle was to shoot José and Erik was to shoot Kitty. Craig told the detectives that Erik told him he and Lyle went into the family room, Lyle pointed his gun at José and shot him. Lyle then went behind José and shot him in the head. Erik told Craig that he was unable to shoot his mother and that when she tried to get away, Lyle shot her. Craig recalled that Erik said, "After it looked like my mother was dead, I shot her twice with my gun." Craig told the detectives that he didn't know whether to believe Erik or not. Zoeller and Linehan were delighted by the details of Craig's story. The only problem came when Craig told the detectives that, "it could have happened." Apparently, Craig and Erik played mind games with one another and Erik saying, "it could have happened," was Erik's way of playing with Craig. After hearing this, the detectives were unsure what to make of Craig's story. Zoeller met with Pam Ferrero, the Los Angeles County deputy district attorney assigned to the case. She told Zoeller that he didn't have enough to file criminal charges yet, but the information he was assembling sounded promising. Another attorney in the district attorney's office suggested that Craig wear a body wire and meet with Erik to get the story on tape. Zoeller didn't think that Craig would do it, but surprisingly Craig agreed to it.

Craig set up a dinner meeting with Erik for November 29. The meeting took place at Gladstone's 4 Fish on Pacific Coast Highway in Pacific Palisades. At the dinner, Erik told Craig that he had been lying and the he and Lyle had nothing to do with their parents' murders.

Although the detectives felt that the meeting between Craig and Erik had been a failure, Pam Ferrero felt otherwise. It convinced her that Craig was telling the truth when he had spoken to the detectives on November 17.

As weeks turned into months, Zoeller, Linehan and Ferrero began to worry. Soon José's estate would be probated and the brothers would wind up with their parents' fortune. The detectives began to search for the shotguns knowing that the shotguns would tie the killers to the crime. Zoeller contacted the Department of Justice for a list of shops selling shotguns in Los Angeles County. He received a list that was 80 pages long. Zoeller did not believe he would find the shop that sold the guns to the brothers. Zoeller believed that Lyle and Erik were clever and probably purchased the guns using one of their friend's names. Zoeller and Linehan searched and searched, but came up with nothing.

On March 5, 1990, the detectives received a break in the case from a woman named Judalon Smyth. Smyth was an attractive 37-year-old woman who owned an audiotape duplicating business. Smyth was also Dr. Jerome Oziel's lover. She told the detectives that Oziel had asked her to eavesdrop on a therapy session he had with the Menendez brothers on October 31, 1989. Smith told the detectives she overheard a shouting match between Lyle and Erik in which Lyle shouted, "I can't believe you told him!" "We've got to kill him and anyone associated with him." According to Smyth, Erik screamed back, "I can't stop you from what you have to do, but I can't kill any more." The session ended when Erik ran out of the office sobbing. Smyth saw Lyle leave the office, followed by Dr. Oziel. Smyth told the detectives that she witnessed Lyle threaten Oziel. Smyth said she heard Lyle say, " I can kind of understand Erik, but he shouldn't have done this..." Oziel asked Lyle if he were threatening him and Lyle shook his hand and said, "Good luck, Dr. Oziel."

Smyth told the police that Oziel continued to have the brothers come in for counseling, telling them that he might be able to help them piece together events in their family's history that had caused them to kill their parents. Smyth also told the detectives that Oziel told her that he had everything on tape, the confessions to the murders and explanations for why the brothers had committed the crimes.

On March 8, 1990, Zoeller obtained a search warrant for Oziel's tapes based on the information that Smyth told him. Oziel handed over 17 audiotapes and seven pages of notes to Zoeller and Linehan. Oziel played portions of the tapes for the detectives and they finally heard the details of what happened on August 20, 1989 from the killers. Afterward the tapes and notes were sealed into a police evidence bag and taken to the Los Angeles County courthouse in Santa Monica. A judge would later rule whether the patient-therapist confidentiality barrier applied to the Menendez brothers.

Arrests

On March 7, Lyle and two of his friends flew from Newark, New Jersey to Los Angeles. Lyle was flying to Los Angeles to try and find the $40,000 Erik had paid to the concert promoter. During the flight, he called Mr. Buffalo's and was told that Detectives Zoeller and Linehan had dropped in an hour after Lyle had left for the Newark airport. According to Glen Stevens, who was sitting next to Lyle on the flight, when Lyle heard about the detectives' visit, he took a money clip out of his pocket and gave him $1,400 and a business card with Gerald Chaleff's name and telephone number on it. Lyle told Glen that if anything happened to him, he should use the money to bail him out of jail. Lyle also said that Chaleff and his therapist, Jerry Oziel, "knew everything."

On March 8, the board of directors of LIVE Entertainment met in Los Angeles to hear an investigative report by the law firm Kaye, Scholer, Fierman, Hays & Handler. The firm hired investigators to examine LIVE's operations to uncover whether there was any reason for stockholders to be concerned about whether the killings could be tied to the company. Pierce

O'Donnell, a partner of the law firm, presented a summary of the investigation to the board of directors. O'Donnell told the LIVE directors that he had learned from the Beverly Hills Police Department that the Menendez brothers were suspects in the killing of their parents. O'Donnell told the board that he believed that the brothers would be arrested soon.

Around 1:00 p.m. on March 8, Lyle and his friends decided to go out for lunch. Lyle's friends jumped into Erik's Jeep while Lyle got behind the wheel. The destination was the Cheesecake Factory, just as on the night of the murders.

Down the street from the Elm Drive mansion, the Beverly Hills police were waiting. The police had decided against surrounding the mansion or storming it by force because Maria Menendez, José's mother, was living there. The police did not want anything to harm her. The police were anxious to arrest Lyle because they had information that he was planning to leave Beverly Hills again. The police would have preferred to arrest Lyle and Erik together, but Erik was in Israel playing in a tennis tournament.

Glen Stevens later recalled that he "thought something was going on" as the Jeep pulled away from the mansion. Stevens saw that a blue Ford with a flashing light had parked across the south end of Elm Drive. Lyle stopped the Jeep just short of running into the blue car. He threw the Jeep into reverse and crashed into a van that had driven up behind the Jeep to block Lyle's retreat.

The police seemed to be everywhere. Someone screamed, "Get out of the Jeep." Lyle and his two friends got out of the Jeep and were handcuffed and taken to the West Hollywood Sheriff's station. Lyle was booked at the station and then transported to the Los Angeles County Men's Jail in downtown Los Angeles.

Later in the afternoon, the Los Angeles County District Attorney, Ira Reiner, held a news conference. Reiner said that the motive for the crime "was greed." Reiner added that, "I don't know what your experience is, but it's been our experience in the district attorney's office that $14 million provides ample motive for someone to kill somebody." Reiner also said, "Special circumstances had been attached to the charges which meant that if convicted, the brothers could be put to death in San Quentin's gas chamber."

The Menendez family took the news of Lyle's arrest hard. Carlos Baralt, Lyle's uncle, said that the "whole family was behind the boys."

There was speculation in the media about whether Erik would flee from Israel, but according to a Menendez family member, Erik was very dependent upon Lyle. According to this relative, "Erik would follow Lyle to hell, even if it meant leaving heaven to do so." After hearing about Lyle's arrest, Erik called his Uncle Carlos from Israel. Baralt told Erik that the best thing for him to do was to turn himself in. Erik flew to Miami to meet his aunt, Marta Cano. Cano notified Zoeller and Linehan that she was flying with Erik from Miami to Los Angeles. On March 11, 1990, Detectives Zoeller and Linehan met Erik and Marta at Los Angeles International Airport. Zoeller immediately took Erik into custody. Erik was booked into the Los Angeles County Men's jail.

Although the brothers had been arrested, Zoeller and Linehan were still building the case against them. The detectives did not have any physical evidence linking the brothers to the murders and continued to search for the store that sold the guns to the brothers. The detectives learned from

Judalon Smyth that Erik had thrown the guns into a canyon off Mulholland Drive. Smyth also told Zoeller that the guns were purchased in San Diego, a place Lyle was familiar with from having played in tennis tournaments held there. Zoeller obtained a list of stores that sold guns in San Diego and started searching. Zoeller believed that the brothers would have selected a smaller store, close to the freeway that runs between Los Angeles and San Diego because they did not know the area well and would not have wanted to get lost. Zoeller checked all the smaller stores and came up empty. In desperation, he began to check the big discount chain stores. On March 14, Zoeller and Edmunds went to the Big 5 store on Convoy Street. When they asked the clerk for the store's firearm records, the detectives found the sale of two Mossberg twelve-gauge shotguns for $199.95 each on August 18, 1989. The form was signed by Donovan Jay Goodreau and listed a San Diego address.

Zoeller called Donovan and asked, "Where were you on August 18, 1989?" Donovan had been at his job, managing a restaurant in New York City. Donovan had punched a time clock and was able to verify that he had in fact been in New York City on August 18, 1989. The address on the form was phony, but the driver's license number on the form matched Donovan's. Donovan was shown a copy of the form and told Zoeller that the signature was not even close to his.

Elliott Alhadeff, the assistant district attorney now assigned to the case, asked the court for an order allowing him to collect handwriting samples from Lyle and Erik to compare to the signature on the firearm form. Erik refused. Zoeller had at last found a physical link between José and Kitty's murders and the Menendez brothers.

Arraignment

Lyle Menendez, second from left, and his brother, Erik, second from right, are flanked by their attorneys Gerald Chaleff, left, and Robert Shapiro, as the brothers delayed entering pleas through their attorneys in Beverly Hills Municipal Court on March 13, 1990

The Andersen and Menendez families retained very good and very expensive legal counsel for Lyle and Erik. Selected to represent Erik was Leslie Abramson, a tiny woman with a Little Orphan Annie hairdo, a vocabulary like a sailor and an unstoppable will. Leslie is the granddaughter of an International Ladies' Garment Workers Union organizer and is so imposing that she intimidates many judges with her fierce presence. She lets her emotions show, if she does not like a judge's ruling, she wrinkles her face and shakes her head, daring the judge to find her in contempt. Leslie is a passionate opponent of the death penalty. She is also very successful too, having only lost one client to a death sentence. The Menendez case would be her fifteenth high profile murder case. She is devoted to her clients, so much so that her devotion to Erik would raise questions about her behavior and ethics during his trial. Abramson's fee for defending Erik was $750,000.

The Menendez brothers were arraigned for the murders of their parents on March 26, 1990 in Judge Judith Stein's courtroom at the Beverly Hills Municipal Court. The brothers entered the courtroom seeming not to care that their lives were on the line.

The brothers had been in the Los Angeles County Men's Jail for two weeks, but neither acted as if they had been in jail at all. Generally, a prisoner is contrite, worried and overwhelmed by court proceedings. The brothers were not contrite. They acted smug and arrogant. The courtroom was filled with reporters and supporters of the brothers, including Jaime Pisarcik and Erik's tennis coach, Mark Heffernan, who had been in Israel with him.

Maria Menendez was also in the audience, supported by a large number of Menendez family members. The brothers waved and smiled at their friends and relatives and acted as if their defense attorneys would quickly clear things up so that the brothers could join their friends and family for a late lunch.

Judge Stein did not seem to be impressed by the two tan young men who sat casually slouched in their chairs before her. She did not seem to appreciate the casual bantering that went on between the men and their attorneys and she did not like the amount of attention the men were paying to their girlfriends, family and friends in the audience.

Stein was a small woman with a nasal voice. She peered out at the brothers through a pair of glasses that sat low on her nose. The brothers apparently found the scene hilarious. Judge Stein ordered the brothers to stand up and face her. They did so and seemed barely able to contain their giggles.

Judge Stein read the charges to the brothers, "You have been charged with multiple murder for financial gain, while laying in wait, with a loaded firearm, for which, if convicted, you could receive the death penalty." "How do you plead?" Erik answered first, almost with a smirk on his face, "Not guilty, your honor." "Not guilty," echoed Lyle. The brothers were held without bail, pending trial, on first-degree murder charges with special circumstances.

Eventually the families retained Jill Lansing to represent Lyle. Lansing is a slender blond woman who had just left the Los Angeles County Public Defender's office to open her own private practice. Unlike Abramson, Lansing was not comfortable in high profile, media-intensive cases. Both Abramson and Lansing hired attorneys to assist them. Abramson hired Marcia Morrissey, forty-three, who had also been a Los Angeles County Public Defender. Morrissey had just finished defending Laney Greenberger in the Cotton Club case. Lansing hired Michael Burt, who was the head trial attorney in the San Francisco Public Defender's office and an expert in death penalty law.

Elliott Alhadeff was to prosecute the Menendez brothers, but he and the District Attorney, Ira Reiner, were not getting along and Reiner replaced Alhadeff and gave the case back to Pam Ferrero. Soon after becoming involved in the case again,

Ferrero married another Assistant District Attorney, Peter Bozanich. Pam Bozanich was thirty-nine and a graduate from Wellesley. Bozanich is a petite woman with dark brown hair with an understated, yet professional air, about her. She was in many ways the complete opposite of Leslie Abramson, who was theatrical and flamboyant. Bozanich had recently prosecuted the retrial of the McMartin Preschool molestation case.

The Tapes

Santa Monica Superior Court Judge James Albrecht ruled that the threats Lyle made to Dr. Oziel erased the patient-therapist confidentiality barrier and ordered that the Oziel tapes be given to the Los Angeles County district attorney's office. There were three tapes at issue. Two of the tapes contained Oziel's dictated notes following the October 31, November 2 and November 28 sessions. The third tape was of the December 11 session, taped with the consent of the brothers' attorney at the time, Gerald Chaleff.

Dr. L. Jerome Oziel

In California, the law protecting the patient-therapist privilege is well established and remains in effect even in situations where a killer confesses to his therapist that he murdered someone. Even in that situation, the privilege guarantees that the therapist cannot go to the police.

If the therapist goes to the police, he can be sued for malpractice. The reason that the privilege is so strong is because the legislature recognizes that in order for psychotherapy to work, a patient must be free to reveal the most intimate details of his life.

There were several hearings about the tapes and after one of the hearings; the sheriff's department announced that they had discovered that the links in Lyle's ankle chain had been cut. To the sheriff's department, this indicated that Lyle was attempting to escape. At another hearing on the tapes, Erik's nose appeared to be swollen and bruised, the result of a jail beating that the sheriff's department said they were investigating.

On August 6, 1990, Albrecht gave the prosecution a major victory. He said that all of the tapes could be used as evidence against the brothers. The judge said, "I have found by a preponderance of the evidence that Dr. Oziel had reasonable cause to believe that the brothers constituted a threat and it was necessary to disclose those communications to prevent the threatened danger." Leslie Abramson promptly appealed the decision to the California Court of Appeals. On March 2, 1991, the California Court of Appeals overturned Albrecht's decision. The prosecutors then filed an appeal with the California Supreme Court.

Part of the Court of Appeals' decision said that Oziel had not acted as a psychotherapist during the last two taped sessions, but acted out of "self-preservation and that the purported therapy was in fact, a charade." The decision quoted freely from the tapes and was released to the public. For the first time, it was revealed that the Menendez brothers had killed their parents. The effect of this revelation on the Menendez and Andersen families ranged from shock to disbelief. Some family members who had been very vocal in their support of the brothers soon dropped out of sight.

On June 4, 1992, the California Supreme Court heard arguments on the issue of the tapes. Leslie Abramson and Michael Burt argued for the brothers saying that only the portions of the tapes that dealt with threats to Oziel should be given to the prosecution. The Court issued its ruling in

August, deciding that the prosecution was entitled to one tape, the tape that was dictated by Oziel dealing with the October 31 and November 2 sessions. The Court decided that the release of the tape was not barred by the patient-therapist privilege because Oziel believed that the brothers had threatened him during the sessions covered on the tape. The Court barred the release of a tape that covered the November 28 session and the December 11 tape made with Chaleff's consent. In those sessions, the Court ruled that there was "insufficient evidence of threats to warrant disclosure of the tape." To the prosecution, the real loss was the December 11 tape of the brothers discussing the murder. The trial could now proceed.

The First Trial

The Menendez brothers spent three years in the Los Angeles County Men's Jail waiting for their trials to begin. The brothers were segregated from other prisoners and housed in separate cells in the jail's 7000 section. This section housed high-profile inmates such as Richard Ramirez, known as the Nightstalker, and O.J. Simpson. They ate their meals in their cells and had an exercise period for one hour three times a week. During the first months of his confinement, Erik was suicidal and received the tranquilizer, Xanax. A priest visited Erik during this time and Erik began to reveal for the first time some of the supposed traumas he suffered during his childhood. It was from these conversations that the foundation was laid for the brothers' controversial defense. In June 1990, Erik began weekly therapy sessions with Dr. William Vicary, a Harvard-trained psychiatrist.

Lyle, during the early part of his confinement, spent a great deal of time on the telephone. He spoke to the manager of Mr. Buffalo's often and this caused other prisoners to complain about the number and length of his telephone calls. Shortly after the sheriff's deputies found Lyle's ankle chains almost cut through, they conducted an inspection of both Lyle and Erik's cells. They found a seventeen-page letter from Lyle to Erik along with some notes in Erik's cell. The notes described plans to travel to South America and then to the Middle East. The deputies also found a drawing of a building with stairwells and doors. Deputies tried to match it to the courthouses that Lyle had been in, but could not find a building that the drawing resembled.

In Lyle's letter he tells Erik that he would never testify against him. Lyle also gives Erik advice that Lyle believes José would have given him. Lyle wrote, "I am not an ordinary person. I do not see things in terms of manslaughter and life terms. I see only win, loss, honor and dishonor. Dad is watching and I will not disappoint him a second time or Mom by giving up and having their deaths be in vain."

According to Pam Bozanich, one day Erik was caught in a sexual embrace with another prisoner. It happened when Erik was being escorted to the shower room with another inmate. The deputy sheriff guarding them propped the door to the shower room open and then went into another room instead of watching Erik and the other inmate. When the guard returned a few minutes later, the door was almost closed and Erik was sitting in a chair with his back to the door. The other inmate was on his knees in front of Erik. When the guard asked what was going on both Erik and the inmate stood up and looked embarrassed.

In the beginning of his confinement, Erik was also visited by his former girlfriend, Janice. To Janice, Erik was growing up fast and becoming a model prisoner. The first time that she had visited Erik, he handed the telephone to Lyle because inmates and visitors were separated by a glass barricade and had to talk to each other using a telephone. Lyle did not talk to her; instead he stood and stared at her breasts as if he had never seen a woman before. Janice felt violated and told Erik never to do that again. According to Janice, Lyle was considered a problem inmate. He monopolized the telephone on his cellblock and on one occasion was accused of stealing food from another inmate on a special diet.

On December 8, 1992, the Menendez brothers were indicted by the Los Angeles County Grand Jury on charges that they murdered their parents.

There were two special circumstances that were attached to the brothers' case which made them eligible for the death penalty: a multiple murder had occurred as the brothers were "lying in wait." A third special circumstance, that the brothers had committed the murders for financial gain, had been thrown out by the grand jury.

The Menendez brothers' trial was held at the Los Angeles County Superior Court located at the San Fernando Valley Government Center in Van Nuys. Judge Stanley Weissberg presided over the trial. Judge Weissberg was in his mid-fifties, wore glasses and had a quiet, scholarly manner about him. In 1992, he had presided over the first Rodney King trial in suburban Simi Valley. That trial had resulted in the deadly Los Angeles riots after four Los Angeles Police Department officers were acquitted.

On May 14, 1993, Judge Weissberg ruled that the cases of Lyle and Erik Menendez would be tried together in the interests of time, cost and convenience. Weissberg saw that there would be an almost complete duplication of witnesses and arguments if separate trials were held for each brother. Weissberg ruled that each brother would have a separate jury. This meant that if evidence that pertained only to Lyle was being heard, Erik's jury would be excluded and vice versa.

The Court summoned 1,100 people for jury duty; eventually two panels of twelve jurors and six alternative jurors were empanelled. Potential jurors were required to complete a 122-item questionnaire. There were 15 questions on the topic of child sexual abuse and violence within families. Lyle's jury was selected first and consisted of seven men and five women. The average age of the jurors was forty-two. Erik's jury consisted of eight men and four women. The average age of the jurors was forty-six.

From the time of the brothers' arrests until shortly before the trial commenced, Leslie Abramson and Jill Lansing had held their cards close to their chests and did not reveal what their defense strategy would be. Bozanich wondered if Abramson and Lansing would use a defense that gambled that the prosecution did not have enough evidence to prove that Erik and Lyle had committed the murders. During a pretrial hearing on June 9, 1993, Abramson said the defense would admit that the brothers had murdered their parents.

The defense would try to prove to the jurors that it was José and Kitty and not Lyle and Erik who should be held accountable for why the murders were committed. Abramson and Lansing would argue that the brothers had been instilled with feelings of fear over a long period of time, going back many years. The athletic, spoiled rich sons who had each at one time in their lives considered becoming professional tennis players; were going to be portrayed as victims of child abuse.

The brothers' defense presented one obstacle: the brothers had never complained to their psychologist or anyone else about abuse, there was no medical evidence of abuse, no photographs of bruises, in other words, no history of abuse at all. If this defense were to succeed, Abramson and Lansing would have to carefully reconstruct specific incidents of abuse that involved Lyle and Erik. In order for the prosecution to prevail, they would have to prove to the jurors that the brothers were liars and that their tales of abuse were not true.

On July 17, 1993, three days before the trial started, Leslie Abramson gave an interview to the *Los Angeles Times*. Abramson said that a series of increasingly intense confrontations between the brothers and their parents had led to the murders. During the interview, Abramson laid out her case which would primarily consist of the defense destroying the image of the Menendez family.

Abramson and Lansing had consulted with Paul Mones, a lawyer and children's rights advocate. Mones had written, *When A Child Kills: Abused Children Who Kill Their Parents*, a book that outlines how attorneys can successfully defend children accused of killing their parents. Mones' book is based on his research, which showed that kids who kill their parents are usually peaceful and have parents that are very private and secretive. Mones found that these children have a low self-opinion of themselves and react only after suffering abuse silently, usually after years of trying unsuccessfully to please their parents. According to Mones, when these children fight back, they strike when their abuser is vulnerable. The crimes tend to be characterized by overkill, instead of one bullet being fired at the abuser, the child will shoot the abuser over and over again. Mones believes that when a parent is murdered, it is their fault.

Abramson and Jill Lansing followed Mones' advice and dressed their clients in boyish sweaters, sport shirts and khaki pants all in an effort to show that Erik and Lyle were not men of 22 and 25, but boys of twelve and fifteen. Abramson wanted to show that Erik was a boy and that she was his indulgent aunt. Throughout the trial she picked lint off his sweater and she made sure to keep her arm on his shoulder whenever she whispered into his ear. By behaving in this way, Abramson implied that she was not defending a monster, just a misunderstood boy who needed good parenting.

The defense also relied on a diagnostic tool developed by therapist E. Sue Bloom for use with incest survivors. The tool is a thirty-four-item checklist that deals with the after effects of childhood sexual abuse. Bloom's checklist had many items that could be applied to both brothers. The checklist contains items such as fear of sleeping alone; blocking out a period of early life; carrying an awful secret; and stealing, all of which Erik admitted to. Lyle's comments fit checklist items, such as: a desire to dissociate from his family; creating a fantasy world, which Lyle did with his stuffed animals; rigid control of thought processes; and, a feeling that there was a demand to achieve in order to be loved.

Both Erik and Lyle had changed dramatically since their arraignment in 1989. At that hearing, they had appeared cocky and arrogant. The brothers had aged and matured in jail. They appeared to have lost weight and Erik, in particular, did not look healthy. His skin was chalk white and he appeared gaunt. Throughout the trial Lyle would wear his hairpiece, but that was about all that remained from his 1989 arraignment.

During the trial, their grandmother, Maria Menendez and their aunts, Marta Cano and Terry Baralt, supported the brothers. Notably absent throughout the trial were members of the Andersen family.

Bozanich came to the trial with some ambivalence, especially concerning the death penalty. Although she believes in the death penalty, Bozanich is aware that many jurors are reluctant to impose it. Lester Kuriyama was not ambivalent about the death penalty when it came to the Menendez brothers. He thought that the brothers were cold, conscienceless killers. In the weeks leading up to the trial, Bozanich had asked Leslie Abramson if she considered asking about a plea bargain, but Abramson never did. The two sides were always too far apart.

Aside from the attorneys and the judge, there was one more entity in the trial: a television camera. Judge Weissberg allowed a single television camera in the courtroom. Weissberg was aware of the intense public interest in the case and the limited number of seats available in his courtroom, so he allowed Court TV to provide a television camera and broadcast the trial.

The trial began on July 20, 1993 with Bozanich's opening statement laying out the case against Lyle. Bozanich described the brutality of the murders: the six wounds to José and the ten wounds to Kitty. She laid the foundation for her theory that the brothers had killed their parents "while lying in wait" as the parents dozed. She described how Lyle had hired bodyguards after the murders because he feared for his own safety. Bozanich told the jury that, "From what we now know, this hint that his own life might have been in danger because of his parents' killings was a lie." Bozanich would often remind the jurors throughout the trial that if Lyle and Erik could lie so frequently and in such detail to avoid being caught, they could also lie about child abuse to avoid death sentences. Bozanich told the jury about the brothers' spending sprees. This was another theme that she would repeat often throughout the trial. She discussed the Rolex watch purchases and Lyle's Porsche, the Marina Towers apartments, Lyle's restaurant and Erik's tennis coach.

Jill Lansing began her opening statement by telling the jurors that Lyle and Erik Menendez killed their parents. Lansing said, "We're not disputing when it happened. The only thing that you are going to have to focus on in this trial is why it happened." Lansing told the jury that, "What we will prove to you is that the murders were committed out of fear." "Fear of two parents who were so brutal, so manipulative, so sexually perverse that they drove their own sons to the most desperate act of defilement." Lansing would not reveal the details of the perversion or the brutality at this point, and went on to describe the lifestyle the brothers enjoyed growing up: Lyle's Afla Romeo, private tennis coaches, luxury vacations and the use of their parents' credit cards. Lansing tried to show that money was not the motive for the murders. Lansing was building up to the heart of the brothers' defense: that the brothers killed their parents because they feared for their lives after confronting their father over a years-long ordeal of sexual, physical and mental abuse. Lansing explained that the "catalyst" for why the murders took place was the fear that the family's old secrets would be revealed and that those secrets would destroy the reputation of "the perfect family."

Lansing told the jury that the catalyst was "Erik's revelation to his brother a few days before the killings that his father had been molesting him for twelve years." This revelation disturbed Lyle "so thoroughly because he, too, had been molested by José from the ages of six to eight." Lansing described how Lyle had confronted José and told him that, "the abuse was going to stop." Lyle told his father that he was "going to let him take his little brother and leave the house." According to Lansing, José told Lyle that "he would do whatever he wanted with his son, and that no one would threaten him." Lansing went on to say that José "made it very clear to Lyle that this secret would never leave the family, and that the people who held the secret and this power over him would not be allowed to live." According to Lansing that is when the brothers drove to San Diego and purchased shotguns using Donovan Goodreau's driver's license. Lansing explained that the murders were a result of what "these children" believed. Lansing's use of the word "children" began a pattern that she and the other defense attorneys would use throughout the trial to refer to the 22 and 25-year-old men.

Lansing told the jury that neither brother had talked about the abuse until after they had been arrested and incarcerated for many months because their shame was so great. The brothers had told a family member about the abuse and that family member had told the defense attorneys. The prosecution was always suspicious of how the abuse was revealed. The prosecutors felt that the timing was curious and that the brothers rehearsed their stories with each other before telling members of their family. The prosecutors believed that the brothers had been visited by a number of psychologists immediately after they were arrested. The psychologists who saw the brothers later, after the stories were revealed to the family, would be the experts to testify at their trial. Lansing also told the jurors that Lyle would testify and describe tales of abuse, including the abuse he began to suffer at age six, when he claimed José began to molest him.

Lester Kuriyama was thirty-nine and although he may be mistaken for a contemporary of Lyle and

Erik's, he was a seasoned prosecutor who held the brothers in greater contempt than Pam Bozanich. He had a deep and emotional hostility toward the brothers and was convinced that they were liars and manipulators who deserved the worst punishment the law provided. Kuriyama never seemed to miss an opportunity to imply that the brothers were a pair of phonies out to con the world.

In his opening statement to Erik's jury, Kuriyama said that the brothers had wanted to "execute their parents and not get caught." Kuriyama told the jurors that Dr. Oziel would describe the confession that Erik had made and how Erik felt that "his father was too controlling." Kuriyama added that "José criticized him and made him feel inadequate and prevented him from doing what he wanted." He told the jury that Oziel would testify that Erik thought that José had disinherited him from his will and that Erik thought that "this was another reason to get rid of José."

Kuriyama explained that Kitty was murdered "because she would have been a witness and would have been miserable and suicidal without José." Kuriyama finished his opening statement by telling the jury that the brothers tried to create a web of deception that included false alibis, lies to the police, a stolen driver's license used to purchase the murder weapons and the employment of a computer expert to delete a computer file.

In her opening statement, Leslie Abramson expanded on many of the same themes that Jill Lansing had outlined during her opening statement to Lyle's jury. Abramson told the jury that "Lyle had acted the way he had to defend his brother." Erik needed to be defended because he was the "real victim in the family." She acknowledged that Erik's revelation of abuse might look suspicious, especially after he had spent time in jail, but it didn't mean that he made it up. Abramson said that the reason that Erik didn't tell the truth earlier was because he did not trust Dr. Oziel or his best friend, Craig Cignarelli. Abramson promised that Erik would tell them "why he killed his parents." She did not say that Erik would tell the truth.

Abramson went on to describe how Erik "was groomed for his father's sexual gratification." She described various acts that Erik alleged were inflicted upon him by José. The defense had won the right to raise issues regarding Kitty's character to the jury. Lansing told Lyle's jury that, "her children were afraid of her, that's why she is dead."

Abramson said that the brothers could not turn to Kitty for "help and solace because all they found was a disturbed woman who dished out more abuse, sexual, physical, and psychological." Weissberg would not allow the attorneys to describe in great detail Kitty's problems with alcohol and prescription drugs, but they could show that Kitty was unstable and obsessive. What the defense was allowed to do, with Weissberg's permission, was to destroy José and Kitty's reputations.

Abramson echoed Lansing's opening statement when she described the week leading up to the murders. Abramson described how Kitty and Lyle had gotten into a screaming fight and how Kitty had reached up and yanked Lyle's hairpiece off his head. Apparently, Lyle had lost most of his hair when he was 14 and wore a toupee because José had once told him that it was better for his image if it appeared that he had a full head of hair. Erik claimed he did not know that Lyle wore a toupee and the shock of this alleged discovery made Erik take Lyle into his confidence.

Erik told Lyle that José had been molesting him for years. This led the brothers to attempt to purchase two handguns, however they told their attorneys they could not purchase the weapons because there was a two-week waiting period. Because the brothers were so fearful and felt they had no time to waste; they drove to San Diego and purchased shotguns. Abramson told Erik's jury how much he looked forward to attending UCLA and moving away from home.

One week before the murders, José told Erik that he would have to sleep at home several days a week so that José and Kitty could keep track of his schoolwork. Abramson said that Erik thought that this meant that the sexual abuse would continue. The defense tried to weave together a seamless story about how and why the murders occurred, but there were some problems. If Kitty and José had intended to kill Lyle and Erik on August 20, why had they invited their friends from Calabasas, Peter and Karen Wiere over to play bridge?

After Abramson had finished her opening statement, Bozanich and Kuriyama reminded the jurors that Erik confessed to Dr. Oziel. Erik had told Oziel about killing José because of José's harsh treatment of him but had never mentioned sexual abuse. The same was true of Erik's confession to Craig Cignarelli. The brothers had never spoken about abuse until they needed a legal defense, almost seven months after they murdered their parents.

During the first phase of the trial, the prosecution called twenty-six witnesses, most were minor participants in the drama of the case. The witnesses ranged from Lyle's bodyguards to the Big 5 store clerk who sold Erik the shotguns and the two computer experts who checked Kitty's computer for an updated will. The prosecution used these witnesses to show that the brothers were accomplished liars, who planned and carried out the murder of their parents.

The prosecution began its case by playing Lyle's 911 call to the Beverly Hills Police Department for the jurors, who now knew that the whole thing was staged. Bozanich wanted the jury to hear for themselves what a good actor Lyle was. Officer Michael Butkus testified that he witnessed the Lyle and Erik run around and yell after the murders, but not cry over the deaths of their parents.

The next witness was the captain of the boat who took the Menendez family shark fishing on August 19, 1989. He described what an odd family they were and how the brothers had spent almost the entire seven-hour trip huddled together at the front of the boat. At the end of the day's testimony, Abramson told reporters that the reason that the brothers had stayed to themselves on the boat was because they feared that "the boat trip was a setup to kill them." To a rational person this sounded rather farfetched considering that there were witnesses on the boat, but Abramson said that Lyle and Erik believed this. Abramson was trying to establish that the brothers had a growing sense of doom leading up to the night of the murders and that they saw the most ordinary actions as potentially life-threatening events.

Les Zoeller described how the brothers returned to the Menendez mansion and the crime scene at 5:30 a.m. on August 21, 1989 and asked for their tennis rackets. Bozanich wanted the juries to see how brazen the brothers were to come back to the crime scene. The brothers were not allowed inside the house because the coroner was examining the bodies of José and Kitty. Leslie Abramson asked Zoeller if he had seen any animal droppings in the house. Zoeller said that he could not remember. Abramson was laying the groundwork for her contention that Kitty was a poor mother and bad housekeeper. The animal droppings would become a running theme during the trial, yet witnesses who had been in the house frequently said that they had never seen any animal droppings.

Sergeant Edmonds testified that he became suspicious of the brothers after Erik told him that when he entered the family room on the night of August 20, he saw and smelled smoke. Edmonds testified that, "I felt that if he smelled smoke, it would have to be pretty rapidly after the shots were fired." Edmonds testified that several of the windows in the family room had been shot out and this would cause the smoke to dissipate quickly.

The prosecution's next witness was a sheriff's weapons expert who demonstrated the operation of a twelve-gauge Mossberg shotgun. The prosecution wanted to show that the murders were premeditated. To fire a Mossberg shotgun, an individual must pull the trigger and go through a two-step pumping process before re-firing the weapon. Abramson objected to the demonstration, but was overruled.

Lyle and Erik's friends had turned on them. Perry Berman, Craig Cignarelli, Donovan Goodreau and Glen Stevens testified for the prosecution. The prosecution used Berman's testimony to show that the brothers had tried to set up an alibi using a witness who never saw anything pertinent to the events on the night of August 20, 1989.

On July 26 Craig Cignarelli testified about his visit to the Menendez mansion twelve days after the murders where Erik described to Craig how "it" happened. This was the first time that the jurors heard Erik's version of the events that occurred in the family room and how it differed from the tale of two terrified young men killing for fear that they were about to be killed. Cignarelli also told the jury that Erik had never told him about any physical, psychological or sexual abuse. At the end of the day, Judge Weissberg ruled that Erik and Craig's screenplay, *Friends*, could not be used as evidence. Weissberg ruled that the screenplay had been written too long before the murders to be relevant.

Donovan Goodreau testified that his wallet with his ID was left behind in Lyle's dorm room at Princeton when he had been forced to leave after being accused of stealing. Donovan also testified that he had once confided to Lyle that he had been molested when he was a little boy. Donovan recalled that Lyle did not respond with any similar stories or remarks about himself and never mentioned being sexually abused during the entire time they were roommates.

Donovan's credibility was challenged when the defense brought up an interview that Donovan had given in March, 1992 to Robert Rand, a freelance writer from Miami, who said he was writing a book about the Menendez case. In that interview, Donovan had mentioned that he heard that José had abused Lyle. Rand gave a copy of the taped interview to a Los Angeles TV reporter who played the tape on the evening news. Bozanich was angry that Rand would inject himself into the trial's proceedings and that Rand appeared on television and accused Donovan of lying. Bozanich believed that Donovan had been "fed" information about José and Lyle and he was repeating a story he had heard.

Glen Stevens followed Donovan and testified that he had heard stories of abuse from Robert Rand and then had repeated those stories to Donovan Goodreau. Stevens's credibility was called into question when Jill Lansing produced his resume and exposed a number of "embellishments" on it: Stevens wrote on his resume that he kept the accounting records for Mr. Buffalo's and claimed the snack shop had sales of one million dollars a year. Stevens admitted that Lyle gave him one of his Rolex watched which he later sold and pocketed the money.

Later in the day, Bozanich questioned Rand. Bozanich pointed out that on the taped interview Donovan never mentioned anything about Lyle and sexual abuse. Bozanich made it appeared that Rand was the source of Donovan's information.

Dr. Irwin Golden, the Los Angeles County assistant coroner, testified about the ten wounds that were inflicted on Kitty and the six inflicted on José. He said that all the wounds occurred in "quick succession."

The prosecution's star witness was Dr. Oziel. Before he took the witness stand, Leslie Abramson promised to "attack his credibility in every way known to man and God." The defense believed that Oziel created the tapes for his own purposes and that Lyle and Erik told Oziel what he wanted to hear. Oziel's credibility was attacked even before he faced Leslie Abramson. On July 23, the California State Board of Psychology filed a complaint that sought to revoke Oziel's license because he had allegedly engaged in "a sexual, social or business relationship with two patients."

On August 4, Dr. Oziel began the first of six days of testimony for the prosecution. Oziel testified before both Lyle and Erik's juries that the brothers wanted to kill José because he was dominating their lives and made them feel inferior. Kitty was murdered because the brothers did not want to leave her behind as a witness. The defense won one battle when Weissberg ruled that Oziel could not use the word *sociopath*. Weissberg considered the word *sociopath* to be a "buzz word" that would be prejudicial to the brothers.

For Bozanich and Kuriyama, Oziel provided the only detailed recreation of the murders, in the brothers' own words. Oziel undermined the defense strategy, which sought to portray the killings as an act of self-defense after years of physical, mental and sexual abuse. Oziel testified that Erik told him that the plan to kill José and Kitty was rooted "in a situation where Erik was watching a BBC television show or movie." Oziel said that Erik told him that José "had just been completely dominating and controlling and was impossible to please." Oziel also testified that the brothers decided to kill their mother because "the brothers did not believe Kitty could have survived emotionally without José." Erik also told Oziel that

"José's near disinheritance of him was an example of why he and Lyle had to kill their father." Oziel described the killings and said that Erik told him that "José and Kitty were 'surprised' when the brothers burst into the family room." Oziel described the threats he had received from Lyle after the October 31 session in which Erik confessed to the murders.

Leslie Abramson and Michael Burt cross-examined Oziel. They brought up his affair with Judalon Smyth and the fact that he had recently settled a lawsuit that she brought against him for $400,000. They also brought up the State Board of Psychology complaint that Oziel improperly prescribed drugs for Smyth and had an improper dual relationship with another patient. In that relationship, Oziel had exchanged therapy sessions for construction work completed around his home.

Before the prosecution rested on August 13, Lester Kuriyama tried to have the "Billionaire Boys Club" miniseries placed into evidence and shown to the juries, but Weissberg ruled against it. To Kuriyama, the miniseries provided the Menendez brothers with a blueprint of how to commit the "perfect murder."

José's former mistress, Louise, followed the trial on Court TV. Louise called Pam Bozanich to say that the man she had known was nothing like the person being destroyed by the defense. She also told Bozanich that Kitty had confronted her about the affair, but rather than behaving like a raving lunatic, as the defense portrayed her, Louise said that Kitty was as pleasant as she could be under the circumstances and just wanted to make sure that the affair was over. Bozanich and Kuriyama debated whether to call Louise to the stand to rebut the portrait that the defense was painting of José, but decided against it because they did not want to subject Louise to an enormous amount of media scrutiny.

The defense intended to call ninety witnesses, but Judge Weissberg ruled that many of the stories that the defense wanted to present were too remote to have "relevance and probative value" which forced the defense to trim its list to 50 witnesses. The defense case lasted three months. The defense had the difficult task of trying to prove to the juries that the brothers were in imminent danger before they killed their parents. Under California law, the "imminent danger" defense was the only way the brothers could be completely acquitted of the murders or had a chance of being convicted of manslaughter.

In order to obtain either of these verdicts, the defense needed to prove two things: that Lyle and Erik had been in fear of their lives and that the conduct of their parents would have produced that same state of mind in a reasonable person. There were two California cases that applied to the Menendez trial and dealt with the battered-wife and the battered child syndromes. *People v. Aris*, was a case where the defendant shot and killed her sleeping husband after being beaten and told by her husband that he would not permit her to live. Aris had been found guilty and the appellate court affirmed the conviction in 1989. The impact of this case was that it placed pressure on judges to permit a wider range of testimony in battered-person cases. Weissberg allowed the defense to present testimony from teachers, coaches, friends, family members and child-abuse experts much to the annoyance of the prosecution, who believed that Weissberg allowed too much of the suspect testimony into the trial. The other case that was relevant to the brothers' defense was *People v. Flannel*, a case where the defendant was convicted of second degree murder in the shooting death of a man with whom the defendant had a history of hostility. This case established the doctrine that an accused person's honest but unreasonable belief, that it is necessary to defend oneself from imminent danger, negates malice aforethought, the mental element that is necessary to convict a person of murder.

Lyle testified over a nine-day period and his testimony was filled with stories about the alleged molestation he suffered from the ages of six to eight and the story that he sexually molested his brother when Erik was five years old. Both Lyle and Erik cried frequently during Lyle's testimony. Lyle testified that at 13, he came to believe that his father was molesting his brother. Lyle testified that his father was so controlling and his mother so emotionally unstable that he sought comfort in his own family of stuffed animals.

Lyle testified that Kitty sexually abused him when he was 11 and 12. He claimed that he would touch Kitty "everywhere" even when his father was sharing the same bed with them. Lyle's testimony was powerful and rich in detail. Lyle's testimony built up to his description of events leading up to the night of the murders and he described shooting his father and then his mother for the jury.

Lyle breaks down testifying about his
abusive father

Jill Lansing asked Lyle why the brothers did not run away from home and Lyle replied that there was no use in doing so because his father was powerful and would have found them. Lyle added that he and Erik believed that the police would not have believed their stories of abuse. Before the defense allowed Lyle to be cross-examined, Lyle admitted offering his girlfriend, Jamie Pisarcik, money if she testified that José had made unwanted sexual advances toward her. Jaime refused and told the police about Lyle's offer of a bribe. In another attempt to thwart questions that might damage Lyle's credibility, Lansing brought up the fact that Lyle had never told Oziel about the sexual abuse. Lyle denied that he had bragged to Oziel about committing "a perfect murder."

Pam Bozanich cross-examined Lyle over a four-day period. She belittled Lyle's account of the killings and challenged him about the alleged abuse, but he did not break down. Bozanich was more successful in identifying inconsistencies in Lyle's version of events. Bozanich was able to have Lyle admit that his parents did not have guns, had made no direct threats to either brother and that parts of his story sounded "awful," and that "a lot of decisions don't make sense."

On September 27, Erik began to testify. Erik's demeanor was ragged and edgy throughout his days on the witness stand. He would stare out from narrow eyes, appearing dangerous and deranged, and a moment later, appear wide-eyed and innocent. Most of the time, he looked more mentally disturbed than sad or remorseful.

Leslie Abramson did not help matters. She stood next to a lectern behind the counsel table and led Erik through his testimony like a drill sergeant. Whenever Erik veered off course or tried to embellish an answer, Abramson interrupted and barked out another question. At times she treated

Erik like a hostile witness, rather than her own client. Abramson's behavior may have been a reaction to the warnings Judge Weissberg had given her during the court session before Erik was to testify. At a sidebar conference, Lester Kuriyama had complained that Abramson had been "caressing and holding Erik in front of the jury." Kuriyama worried that this behavior made Erik appear childlike and innocent. Weissberg warned Abramson "the conduct of counsel in touching and physically reacting to the defendants is an area of concern." He told Abramson, "counsel are to be acting as professionals, not nursemaids or surrogate mothers."

Erik testified that he believed that his parents would kill him. He also said that Kitty seemed to have magical powers, she knew where he went, who his friends were, everything he did. Erik's statements seemed difficult to believe, especially from a 22-year-old man. This was part of the defense's attempt to show that Lyle and Erik had been infantilized by their father's control and that neither brother was the age they appeared to be. Erik testified about killing his parents and the sexual abuse he allegedly suffered at José's hands. At one point in his testimony, Erik volunteered that he began to put cinnamon in his father's tea and coffee because he had heard from classmates that it made semen taste better. It seems difficult to believe that this actually occurred because cinnamon has a distinctive taste that José would have noticed.

Lester Kuriyama repeatedly tried to bring up the issue of Erik's sexuality, but Judge Weissberg refused to allow it. Kuriyama felt that it was relevant because the defense was trying to make it appear that José was a sexual predator. One witness had testified to seeing gay porn magazines in the house, the implication being that they belonged to José, which could substantiate the claim that José had enjoyed sex with men. However, if the magazines belonged to Erik, this would cast the issue in an entirely different light.

Under cross-examination, Erik seemed to have difficulty remembering details. Lester Kuriyama asked Erik questions about the killing of his parents and Erik answered many of Kuriyama's questions with an "I don't remember." Kuriyama caught Erik in the biggest lie of the trial when he had Erik describe in meticulous detail the attempted purchase of two handguns on Friday, August 18, 1989. Erik testified that he and Lyle had driven to a Big 5 store in Santa Monica and had looked at an assortment of handguns. Erik described how the handguns were displayed in a glass case, how he selected two handguns and how he could not complete the purchase because California had a fifteen-day "cooling off" period. Because the brothers believed that their lives were in imminent danger, they could not wait and did not purchase the weapons.

Kuriyama asked Erik, "now, you're telling the truth about everything in this case, aren't you?" Erik answered, "I'm telling you the truth to the best that I can." Kuriyama asked Erik, "Did you truly go to the Santa Monica Big 5 store on the morning of August 18 to buy these handguns?" Erik answered, "Definitely. Without a doubt I did." Then Kuriyama dropped a bombshell. "Mr. Menendez, did you know that Big 5 stopped carrying handguns in March of 1986?" This was a lie of huge proportion. Erik fumbled for a response. "No, I don't know that. Mr. Kuriyama, there were guns there and we did look at them, and he did say we could not carry them anymore."

This was not the only inconsistency that Kuriyama caught Erik in. When Kuriyama questioned Erik about the television miniseries, the "Billionaire

Boys Club," Erik denied that he had seen it. Erik also admitted that he did not think his parents would have disinherited him. Up to this point in the cross-examination, Erik had testified that he thought his parents were. After Kuriyama finished his cross-examination, Leslie Abramson tried to pick up the pieces. Erik told the court that he couldn't remember which Big 5 store he and Lyle had visited.

On October 14, the defense began a new phase of its case by attempting to explain for jurors why Lyle and Erik Menendez could have believed that their lives were in immediate danger, even though their parents were not armed. Ann Tyler, a Salt Lake City psychologist, was the first in a string of experts to testify. Tyler testified that the Menendez brothers suffered from a condition called "learned helplessness" that occurs as a result of intense, repeated abuse. Tyler testified that she had no doubt that José and Kitty Menendez had psychologically abused their young sons in virtually every way possible. Bozanich cross examined Tyler and noted that many of the worst anecdotes about the family were totally uncorroborated. Tyler noted the naivete of the brothers, which came across frequently when they testified and in completely accidental ways that, unlike crying, they would have difficulty faking. There was a softness, a "hothouse plant delicacy" to them, even when they were caught off guard by a question and responded in a flash of anger that they quickly covered up. There was also the bizarre respect and love for their father, even though they had killed him, and that too, seemed genuine.

During this time, Kitty's family began to speak to the news media about the defense and how she was being portrayed. Kitty's brother, Milton Andersen, told his hometown paper, *The Daily Southtown,* that the brothers' defense was "bull." He believed that Lyle and Erik killed because of greed. He said that the defense visited him and tried to convince him that his sister and brother-in-law were bad people. Andersen told the paper: "my sister didn't abuse her children." Andersen felt that José and Kitty had not disciplined their sons enough.

Ann Burgess was the second defense expert to testify. Burgess is a professor of psychiatric mental health nursing at the University of Pennsylvania and an expert in crime scene analysis. She examined the crime scene pictures of the Menendez family room and testified that it was a "disorganized" crime scene and could not have been the product of a premeditated murder. She also testified that the random nature of the wounds led her to believe that there was an overkill element of the crime and this showed a lack of planning.

On October 21, Jill Lansing's first expert witness testified. Stuart Hart, an Indiana University professor, testified about his belief that Lyle had been severely mistreated psychologically.

Jon Conte was Lansing's next expert. He testified that he interviewed Lyle in jail for 60 hours during 1993 and believed he was telling the truth about the abuse because of the "affect" that Lyle had. The "affect" was shame and a reluctance to talk about the abuse because it was embarrassing.

Bozanich felt confident that the jurors did not believe the defense's expert witnesses or the brothers' stories of abuse. She was so confident that she decided not to call her psychological expert, who had sat through much of the early portion of the trial. This may have been her biggest mistake during the trial.

One of the last defense witnesses called was Dr. Kerry English, the medical director of the child abuse team at Martin Luther King Hospital in south central Los Angeles. He testified that he found no evidence that Erik had been sodomized, although physical evidence of molestation is rare. Dr. English had reviewed Erik's medical records from the time he was a child and found a curious reference to a 1977 injury. The notion in Erik's medical file read, "hurt posterior pharynx, uvula and soft palate healing well." Dr. English was asked if such an injury to the back of the throat could be caused by child abuse and he answered, "Yes, oral copulation." There are also other things that can cause such an injury, a Popsicle stick, for instance, during a fall. This injury was suspicious and the first physical evidence on the issue of abuse. All of the other abuse testimony had come from the brothers or from friends or family members who said they were given the information from the brothers. On cross-examination, Bozanich was able to have Dr. English admit that there were other things that could cause injuries to the back of the throat.

Ed Fenno had been a houseguest of the Menendez family. He testified that José had been disappointed when Erik had turned down the opportunity to attend UC Berkeley in favor of

UCLA. José thought that Berkeley was a better school academically than UCLA and was disappointed by Erik's decision. Erik preferred UCLA because it had a better tennis team. Fenno's testimony showed that Erik had made the decision to attend UCLA on his own. Bozanich asked Fenno if he ever saw Erik lie to his parents and Fenno answered that "it was somewhat common for both brothers to lie."

The defense played the December 11 confession tape for the jurors after Judge Weissberg ruled that the defense had waived the patient-therapist privilege because they had made the mental state of the brothers an issue during the trial when they claimed that the brothers killed out of fear. On the tape, Lyle can be heard discussing the reasons that his parents were killed. Lyle had bragged on the tape that he and Erik had "shown great courage by killing their mother." Lyle had also said, "he missed having these people around. I miss not having my dog around. If I can make such a gross analogy." There was a chilling, monotone quality to Lyle's voice; it was empty and hollow. On the tape there was no reference to sexual abuse. José had to be killed because he was controlling the brothers' lives and was a bad husband. Erik does not say much on the tape, but can be heard crying in the background.

Judalon Smyth was called by the defense to discredit Oziel's testimony and testified for two days. Smyth's testimony revolved around two themes: Oziel had manipulated and bullied her into a relationship and many of her earlier statements about what she knew about Lyle and Erik were mistaken. Smyth's own credibility was questionable. She had given a long affidavit to the police and had testified behind closed doors before Judge Albrecht on the admissibility of the tapes. She had also appeared on television.

Bozanich was angry that Smyth was recanting her earlier statements. Bozanich believed that Smyth was angry at the district attorney's office for not filing rape charges against Oziel. Bozanich had referred Smyth to the D.A.'s sex-crimes division, which had rejected the case because of insufficient evidence.

Bozanich cross-examined Smyth about the different versions of the story she had told and Smyth answered that she was not responsible for her earlier answers because Oziel had brainwashed her. By the time her testimony ended, it appeared that jurors had a difficult time believing Smyth. Smyth was the last of fifty-six witnesses called by the defense.

The aim of the prosecution's rebuttal witnesses was to contradict the stories told by the brothers about the days leading up to the murders and to rehabilitate the reputations of José and Kitty. One rebuttal witness who testified was Grant Walker, a man who cleaned pools for a living. He testified that he was at the Menendez mansion, fixing the switch on the automatic spa control on Saturday, August 19, the day before the murders. Walker said that he saw Lyle playing tennis with another man, while Erik stood next to José and Kitty who were seated at a patio table pulled up to the tennis court. Walker testified that he witnessed Kitty speaking to Lyle about his tennis game. Lyle responded "in anger," and used a vulgarity. Walker said that Erik also seemed angry with his parents. This exchange occurred around 2:00 p.m. in the afternoon. This was powerful evidence. According to the stories that the Menendez brothers had told, they had purposely stayed away from the house because they feared their parents.

Flor Suria was the Menendez family housekeeper and had slept in the mansion Monday through

Friday during the time she was employed by the family. She testified that she never saw Kitty or José yelling at the brothers. Suria also testified that she did not hear Lyle cry as his toupee was allegedly pulled off on Tuesday and that she did not hear any other noise from the fight that José was supposed to have had with Erik on Thursday before the murders occurred.

Jamie Pisarcik testified that she had been Lyle's girlfriend off and on for about three years. The relationship continued after Lyle was arrested until one day in December 1990 when Jaime, having grown suspicious of Lyle, asked him to tell her the truth. Jaime testified that Lyle told her that he had lied to her and that the truth was that he had killed his parents. The reason for the murders was that José had been molesting Erik and that Kitty had molested Lyle. Jaime told Lyle that she did not believe him and shortly after this exchange took place they had broken up. Jaime also testified that in 1987 she had gone with Lyle to purchase a toupee in Birmingham, Alabama and that she and Erik had a conversation about the toupee in 1988. This was another hole in the defense case. Erik had testified that seeing Lyle without his toupee shocked him into confessing the molestation and this had led to the killings. Jill Lansing attacked Pisarcik's credibility and portrayed her as a gold digger that dreamed about marrying into a wealth family, only to have those dreams destroyed when her fiancé admitted that he was a killer.

Kitty's brother, Brian Andersen, testified that Erik was not timid and appeared to him to have "a puffed up ego." Both brothers were not reluctant to use vulgar language when talking to their parents or to spend their parents' money. José had told Andersen that Lyle had to learn to support himself, that he and Kitty were not going to pay his way forever. The defense countered Andersen's testimony by showing that he had an interest in Kitty's estate and had filed a document in probate court claiming his family would stand to inherit if it were proven that Kitty died after José.

Marlene Eisenberg, José's secretary for fourteen years, testified about Lyle and Erik's behavior after their parents' memorial service. Eisenberg had ridden in the limousine with the brothers after the memorial service. Lyle asked Eisenberg, "Who said I couldn't fill my father's shoes?" Eisenberg told Lyle to "make your own tracks in life and don't try to fill his shoes." Lyle then extended a tasseled loafer and said, "You don't understand. These are my father's shoes."

The defense called Dr. Vicary as a witness to counter the rebuttal witnesses and support the validity of the alleged abuse. Vicary testified that Erik was a "basket case, pathetic, wimpy, a hopeless mess" when he first met him in jail. Erik had told Vicary about the molestation in August 1990, after Erik had undergone months of therapy and was taking antidepressant medication and tranquilizers. Rather than question Vicary's opinion of Erik's mental state and the issue of abuse, Bozanich asked Vicary how much he had earned from his work on the case. Bozanich asked if the reason that Erik was so upset in jail was because he was facing murder charges and Vicary said no and that he was quite shocked to see that Erik "liked it in jail." Vicary added that Erik, "found for the first time in his life there was no pressure on him."

Mark Heffernan was the last witness who testified at the trial. He was called by the defense to lessen the testimony of the pool man, Grant Walker, who testified that he saw the Menendez brothers on the afternoon of August 19 playing tennis at the mansion. Heffernan testified that he was the brothers' tennis coach during the summer of 1989 and denied being at the Menendez mansion that day.

Before closing arguments began, Judge Weissberg gave the prosecution another victory when he declined to give the juries an instruction that could have led to an acquittal. Weissberg said that there was "simply no evidence" that an average person would have been in fear of his life, as the brothers said they were, given the events that occurred on August 20, 1989. Weissberg would have allowed the juries to consider a manslaughter verdict.

Michael Burt began his closing argument by telling Lyle's jurors that they must consider that the murders were carried out while the brothers were in a state of "fear and panic that followed year after year of abuse by bullying parents." Burt said that Lyle was operating like an "unthinking robot" on the night of August 20, 1989 and that he shot his parents on "instinct" and not as part of a carefully thought out plan. Burt argued that the circumstances under which the murders took place did not meet the legal standards for first degree murder.

Bozanich responded by stating that "this is not a complicated case. These two people were watching TV and they got slaughtered by their sons." She challenged Burt's idea that the brothers did not plan the murders, pointing out that they drove to San Diego to purchase shotguns. Bozanich also quoted from the transcript of the Oziel session where Lyle said that there would be "no way" he would have carried out the shootings alone and had decided to let Erik "sleep" on the plan.

Jill Lansing walked the jurors through the crime and asked them to consider "the entire event, dating back to Lyle's childhood sexual molestation."

Bozanich was sarcastic and biting in her closing statement. She called Lyle and Erik "spoiled, vicious brats" who got the "best defense Daddy's money could buy." At one point, Bozanich said of the defense, "For all those children who were severely abused and who became useful members of society, this defense is an offense."

During her three day closing argument, Abramson explained away problems with the defense, accused prosecution witnesses of being liars, publicity seekers and attacked Dr. Oziel. Toward the end of her argument, Abramson finally did something that the prosecution had hoped Erik would have done three years earlier; she broke ranks with Lyle. She told the jurors that "I don't want Erik to be taking the rap for Lyle" and added, "the evidence in this case does not prove that Erik killed anybody."

Lester Kuriyama's final argument was completed in three hours. He told the jury that he would not attempt to "dazzle" them, but instead asked the jury to "base your decision in this case on common sense." He told the jury that Erik was homosexual and the reason he raised this issue was that "if the defendant were engaging in consensual sex with other men that would account for him being able to describe what he described for you, his sexual encounters with his father." Kuriyama went on the tell the jury that José had not forced Erik into homosexual acts, but was in fact furious that Erik was gay.

Judge Weissberg gave Lyle and Erik's juries four choices in deciding the brothers' fate. The juries could find the brothers guilty of first-degree murder with special circumstances; they could find the brothers guilty of second-degree murder; they could find the brothers guilty of voluntary manslaughter; or they could find the brothers guilty of involuntary manslaughter. Lyle and Erik each faced sentencing on three counts: the murder of José, the murder of Kitty and the charge of conspiracy to commit murder.

On January 13, 1994, after 16 days of deliberation, Erik's jury announced that it was deadlocked and unable to reach agreement on any of the counts. On January 25, after deliberating for 24 days, Lyle's jury announced that it was deadlocked. The juries for both brothers were polarized over whether the brothers were killers or long suffering victims of abuse. Judge Weissberg declared mistrials in both cases.

The outcomes of the cases were a victory for the defense. Only three of the jurors on Lyle's jury voted for the most serious charge of first degree murder in the shooting of his father, José, while five did so on Erik's jury.

Gil Garcetti, the District Attorney who replaced Ira Reiner, said that the Menendez brothers would be retried and that he "would rather have a hung jury than a manslaughter verdict because this is a murder case."

The People vs. Lyle and Erik Menendez was never about guilt or innocence, the defendants admitted that they killed their parent in cold blood and showed neither mercy nor remorse. What the trial was about was the sons' refusal to accept personal responsibility for their own acts. Instead they blamed their parents for an endless catalog of abuse that transformed the victims into the killers. The state attempted to prove that the defendants killed out of hatred and greed, and were lying sociopaths who invented the sensational allegations of sexual, psychological and physical abuse against their parents.

Although the case against the Menendez brothers appeared to be a "slam dunk" murder prosecution, it was derailed by carefully rehearsed testimony, great defense attorneys, prosecutors that were caught by surprise, an indecisive judge and a group of jurors manipulated to accept an outlandish defense. The result was a mistrial that some thought was a miscarriage of justice.

The Second Trial

On February 28, 1995, Judge Weissberg set a trial date of June 12, 1995 for the retrial of the Menendez brothers. The retrial was postponed a number of times and began in August 1995. In April 1995, Judge Weissberg ruled that the brothers would be retried together, in front of a single jury. Weissberg ruled that the advantages of a "single trial greatly outweigh the potential prejudice."

For the retrial, David Conn, a veteran Los Angeles County assistant district attorney, and Assistant District Attorney Carol Najera replaced Pam Bozanich and Lester Kuriyama. Conn had 18 years of experience and was acting head deputy of the major crimes unit of the Los Angeles County district attorney's office. Conn dropped out of high school at the age of 17, joined the Marines, and was sent to Vietnam. He eventually graduated from college and law school. Conn is smooth, impeccably dressed and is often compared to comic hero, Clark Kent, to whom he bears more than a passing resemblance. Conn spent two and one half years mapping out the strategy he would use to dismantle the Menendez defense.

Leslie Abramson continued to represent Erik, although she was paid by the taxpayers of Los Angeles County because the Menendez estate had run out of money. Abramson was assisted by Barry Levin, a Los Angeles criminal defense attorney. The Los Angeles County Superior Court declared both Lyle and Erik indigent. Lyle qualified for representation by the public defender's office. Jill Lansing no longer represented Lyle and was replaced by Charles Gessler, a Los Angeles County Public Defender, who was considered the dean of the death penalty bar. This would be Gessler's last case before retiring. Gessler was assisted by deputy public defender, Terri Towery.

On August 21, 1995, jury selection began in the retrial of the Menendez brothers. On October 11, 1995, opening statements began. Judge Weissberg ruled that the trial would not be televised because it would "increase the risk that jurors would be exposed to information and commentary about the case outside of the courtroom." Weissberg also limited the number of witnesses the defense was able to call regarding the allegations of abuse. During the retrial, 64 witnesses testified. This was in contrast to the first trial where 101 witnesses testified. The retrial lasted 23 weeks and more closely resembled a regular murder trial: somber, gruesome, and occasionally dull rather than the media spectacle of the first trial.

During the two and one half years between trials, Conn studied the mistakes made by Bozanich and Kuriyama to make sure he did not repeat the biggest mistake of the first trial Bozanich's decision not to address head-on the brothers' allegations of years of physical, emotional and sexual abuse. Bozanich and Kuriyama had ignored it all, guessing incorrectly that jurors would too. The prosecution hired Dr. Park Elliott Dietz, a well-known forensic psychiatrist, to assist them.

Conn presented a new theory about the way in which the killings were carried out. Conn decided not to call Dr. Oziel to testify and instead planned to play a tape of the brothers confessing to the murders. Conn vigorously attacked the defense theory that the brothers suffered from battered person's syndrome and was successful in having Judge Weissberg rule that the defense could not present this theory to the jury. At the first trial, Bozanich believed that this defense applied to the brothers.

In his opening statement, Conn argued that the Menendez brothers were motivated by greed when they ambushed their parents. Conn illustrated his points by showing jurors autopsy and crime scene photographs. Conn said that the brothers "were carrying their dead parents' safe to the home of a probate attorney" 24 hours after they murdered their parents. Conn argued that the brothers were trying to get their hands on their parents' money as fast as they could.

Leslie Abramson countered that the brothers killed out of "mind-numbing, adrenaline-pumping fear" that their parents would kill them for threatening to expose the family's secrets.

Abramson told the jury that "we will prove to you that Erik was tortured, terrorized, exploited, molested and abused to such a state he lived in a constant state of fear."

Charles Gessler told the jurors that the brothers believed that their parents had supernatural powers and "knew everything" about their sons' activities. Gessler argued that the prosecution's theory that the brothers wanted their parents' money was wrong because Lyle and Erik thought that their parents' had disowned them.

Conn began the prosecution's case by playing three tapes that incriminated the brothers. The first tape Conn played was of the brothers being interviewed by members of the Beverly Hills Police Department. The interview took place one month after the murders and the brothers were heard saying that they had not had any problems with their parents and discussing their activities on the day of the murders. Conn next played the tape of the brothers admitting to Oziel that they killed their parents. The last tape Conn played was of Lyle's 911 call to the Beverly Hills Police Department on the night of August 20, 1989. Conn told the jury that the brothers "had spun a web of lies after the killings and turned to tears" so they would not be suspected.

Perry Berman's testimony was similar to that of his testimony during the first trial. He testified that José was critical of Lyle's taste in women and was a strict parent. Judge Weissberg limited the scope of Terri Towery's cross-examination, throwing out as irrelevant some questions that probed recollections that cast José in a negative light.

During the second week of trial, the prosecution presented evidence to support its theory that greed motivated the brothers to kill their parents. Klara

Wright, the wife of a probate attorney that the brothers retained, testified that the brothers brought a safe to their home hoping to find a copy of their parent's will inside. Wright had not testified at the brothers' first trial because the prosecutors did not know about the safe until after the first trial was over. The safe was opened two days after the murders when Brian Andersen and Carlos Baralt, the brothers' uncles could be present. The safe was empty.

Carlos Baralt testified that two months before the murders, José told him that he wanted to disinherit his sons. Conn asked Baralt if he knew of any evidence that José sexually abused his sons and Baralt answered no. On cross examination, Baralt was asked by Leslie Abramson why José had talked about disinheriting his sons and Baralt answered that José was disappointed that Lyle was failing academically at Princeton and that in José's opinion, Erik lacked talent, toughness and forcefulness.

During the third week of the trial, Conn announced that Dr. Irwin Golden, the coroner who performed the autopsies on José and Kitty would not testify at the trial. Golden had testified at the first trial that he could not say for certain how many shots were fired or the sequence of shots that killed the couple. In 1995, Golden was heavily criticized for the mistakes he made in the autopsies on Nicole Brown Simpson and Ronald Goldman and was not called by the prosecution in the O.J. Simpson case because of those mistakes. Conn had Dr. Roger McCarthy reconstruct the shootings. Using his reconstruction, McCarthy was able to determine the sequence of shots and showed that the murders were premeditated and deliberate.

The prosecution attacked the credibility of the brothers by introducing portions of a letter that Lyle had written in July 1991 to Amir (Brian) Eslaminia, a potential defense witness. The letter asked Eslaminia to testify falsely that the brothers had asked him to loan them a handgun. Eslaminia was a former classmate of Erik Menendez at Beverly Hills High School. Neither the letter nor Eslaminia played a role in the first trial because the police learned about Eslaminia and the letter in 1995. In 1984, members of the "Billionaire Boys Club" murdered Eslaminia's father as part of an extortion plot. His brother Reza was imprisoned for his role in the crime. Gessler told the jury that Lyle did not go through with the plot. Abramson tried to show that Erik had nothing to do with Lyle's plan.

Conn called a private pathologist, Robert Lawrence, to support the prosecution's new theory of the crime scene. The prosecution believed the Lyle and Erik executed their parents and then shot them in the leg in order to make the murders appear to be organized crime hits. Lawrence illustrated his testimony with wooden mannequins pierced with wooden rods to demonstrate his conclusions regarding the angles of the shotgun blasts. Lawrence testified that José was struck four times and Kitty was struck nine times with shotgun blasts and that they were shot in the head and extremities, but were not shot in their torsos. Lawrence also testified that José was seated on the sofa when he was shot and that the wound to his thigh was inflicted after he had died. The fatal shot was fired at point blank range to the back of José's head.

Most of the shots to Kitty occurred when she was lying on the floor and that some of shots to Kitty's arms, hand and shoulder indicated that she might have been cowering. Abramson tried to show that the blood patterns on the shirt José was wearing indicated that the shots might not have been fired in the direction that Lawrence claimed they were.

Roger McCarthy of Failure Analysis Associates reconstructed the August 20, 1989 murders, shot by shot, and showed the jurors a computer-generated recreation of the murders. McCarthy was the prosecution's star witness and testified that the brothers surprised their parents as they sat in front of the television set in the family room. McCarthy testified that José and Kitty were sitting side by side on a sofa when they were attacked and that the brothers aimed "kneecapping" shots at their parents to make the killings look like a Mafia hit. The brothers maintained throughout their trial that their parents were standing when the shooting began.

Gessler questioned McCarthy about his qualifications to examine the Menendez murder scene. McCarthy testified that he had never visited a crime scene or witnessed an autopsy and that he had never seen the impact of a gunshot wound on a human body. He also conceded that he did not consult with the coroner or criminalist before reaching his conclusions about the Menendez murders.

On November 20, Conn rested the state's case against the Menendez brothers. He had called 30 witnesses. The cornerstone of the state's case was McCarthy's computer generated reconstruction of the August 20, 1989 murders of José and Kitty Menendez. Conn used the reconstruction to demonstrate to the jurors that the brothers had deliberately and methodically killed their parents. The reconstruction was strongly disputed by the defense and contradicted by the brothers' testimony in the first trial, where the brothers testified that they fired their shotguns in a blind panic.

The defense began its case by calling Martin Fackler, an expert on wound ballistics. Fackler testified that the McCarthy reconstruction could not be considered scientific because it contained too many errors. Fackler said that no one could design a reconstruction of the Menendez crime scene because there were too many variables. Under Conn's cross-examination, Fackler, demonstrated that he did not know the facts of the Menendez case as well as McCarthy.

During Abramson's redirect examination of Fackler, she told the jury about the defense's newest version of events that occurred on August 20, 1989. Abramson said that the brothers had entered the family room and that José and Kitty were standing in front of the couch, facing them. Erik began to shoot randomly at his parents. Lyle was to Erik's right and began to fire his shotgun as he walked around the room. Lyle fired the contact wound to José's head. Abramson did not describe the shooting of Kitty, but said that she was standing as the shots were fired.

Abramson called Ron Linhart, the assistant director of the Los Angeles Sheriff's Department crime lab, to rebut the conclusions reached by Roger McCarthy. Linhart testified that his blood spatter analysis contradicted much of McCarthy's reconstruction and that his analysis showed that José and Kitty must have been standing at some point during the shootings.

Dwight Van Horn testified as a defense witness. At the first trial, he had testified as a prosecution witness about the type of shotguns used in the killings. Van Horn testified that McCarthy's reconstruction was "junk science" because it "ignored evidence in some instances and lacked it in others." Conn attacked Van Horn and suggested that he resented the prosecutors using McCarthy's firm instead of the sheriff's department for the crime scene reconstruction.

Dr. Cyril Wecht, a well-respected pathologist from Pennsylvania, testified for the defense that any "reconstruction of the shootings was doomed to failure," because the victims and the defendants were all moving during the killings. Charles Morton testified that the blood patterns and shotgun pellet holes in the clothing of José and Kitty contradicted the prosecution's reconstruction of the crime scene. Morton testified that the physical evidence at the crime scene indicated that Kitty was standing when she was shot. Morton further testified that the blood patterns on and around the family room couch and on José's clothing indicated that he had been shot while standing, except for the shot to the back of his head.

On December 6, Erik began the first day of 15 days of testimony. Erik's testimony began much like it did in the first trial where he described details of the alleged sexual abuse José supposedly inflicted on him. Under Barry Levine's guidance, Erik testified that his parents were violent: Kitty humiliated and degraded him and José beat and molested him. Erik told the jury that he loved his parents and that he did not kill them out of hatred or for money or because of abuse. Erik testified that the brothers feared their parents would kill because they threatened to reveal the alleged sexual abuse.

During the third day of Erik's testimony, Judge Weissberg limited his testimony about allegations of early childhood abuse. The judge rejected as irrelevant some of the stories the defense wanted to introduce. The judge also limited testimony that had little to do with the brothers' state of mind at the time they killed their parents. The defense argued that the brothers' early childhood trauma was critical for the jury to hear so that they could understand why the brothers thought their parents were planning to kill them.

Erik testified that José had told him that he had been written out of his will because he was not living up to José's expectations. Erik also testified about the circumstances leading up to the taped confession at Oziel's office.

Conn set out to portray Erik as a liar. Conn pointed out to the jury that Erik had lied for six months to the police, his family and friends about the murders before he and Lyle were arrested. Conn attacked Erik's claims that his father had forced sex upon him at the age of 18 when Erik had a car and money to leave his parents' home. Conn asked Erik why he did not join the Army and Erik said that the Army would not have protected him from his father because his father "was the most powerful man I've ever met." Erik later conceded that there were no living witnesses to the sexual abuse. Conn raised the issue of Erik's sexual orientation to show that it was a source of tension in the Menendez family.

Because Erik had "tendered his mental state" as part of his defense, Judge Weissberg ruled that Erik had to undergo a psychological examination by Dr. Dietz. Prior to his involvement in the Menendez case, Dietz had testified in numerous high-profile trials. His critics say that he is biased in favor of the prosecution. Dietz has assisted many prosecutors in winning convictions against defendants such as Betty Broderick, who fatally shot her ex-husband and his second wife, and serial killer Jeffrey Dahmer.

On January 9, 1996, Erik completed his testimony by attempting to explain questions raised by the prosecution during his eight days of cross-examination. Erik said that he and his brother did not concoct stories of child abuse in order to avoid murder convictions.

Dr. John Wilson, a psychology professor from Cleveland State University, testified that Erik suffered from Post-Traumatic Stress Disorder at the time he killed his parents. Wilson testified that the cause of Erik's disorder was the repeated acts of sexual, physical and psychological abuse that he experienced. Wilson said that Erik suffered from the classic symptoms of Post-Traumatic Stress Disorder that included nightmares and amnesia. This was the first time that jurors had heard a specific diagnosis applied to Erik Menendez. Wilson did not testify at the first trial.

On January 12, Charles Gessler completely changed the direction of Lyle's defense. Gessler told the court that he planned to argue that Lyle killed his parents in the heat of passion, that fear and anger overwhelmed him on August 20, 1989 when he and Erik murdered their parents. During the first trial, Lyle had testified that he killed his parents out of the honest and mistaken belief that his parent were going to kill him and that he was afraid for his life. Gessler now told the jury that Lyle was a reasonable man who reacted out of fear, anger and passion. At the first trial, the defense used the "imperfect self-defense theory" and argued that the brothers could not be judged by the standard of what a reasonable person would do because years of abuse caused the brothers to see danger differently than a normal person.

The reason that Lyle's attorneys changed defense strategies was that Lyle did not want to testify because of damaging impeachment evidence the prosecution had gathered since the first trial. Lyle was considered a sympathetic witness during the first trial, however prosecutors had tape recorded conversations between Lyle and Norma Novelli, Lyle's one-time confident, where Lyle describes how he "snowed" the jury at his first trial with his testimony about abuse. The prosecution also discovered a letter Lyle had written to a former girlfriend instructing her on how to testify at the first trial. Because Lyle did not testify, his attorneys were not able to call child abuse experts to testify about his state of mind. Without Lyle's testimony, he was not able to use the same defense as he had in his first trial.

At the beginning of the trial, the brothers had mounted a joint defense. However, as the trial wore on, Gessler relied almost completely on Abramson's witnesses and called very few on behalf of Lyle. As a result, Lyle remained somewhat of an enigma to the jury.

Toward the end of the defense case, Judge Weissberg ruled that six witnesses who had testified at the first trial were irrelevant to the second trial and would not be allowed to testify. Weissberg ruled that the parents' alleged psychological mistreatment of the brothers was irrelevant.

On January 30, after presenting 25 witnesses, the defense rested. Judge Weissberg limited the number of mental health experts the defense was allowed to present. In the first trial, the defense presented five experts. At the second trial, the defense was allowed to present only one. In addition, the defense was not allowed to present the testimony of Dr. William Vicary, the psychiatrist who had treated Erik since 1990.

The prosecution began its rebuttal on February 5, 1996. Jaime Pisarcik testified that Erik knew that Lyle wore a toupee as early as 1988. Pisarcik's testimony called into question a major part of the defense's case that a number of confrontations between José and Kitty and Lyle and Erik lead to the murders on August 20, 1989.

Dietz testified that Erik did not suffer from any disorder that would impair his ability to make rational decisions on the night that he murdered his parents. Dietz diagnosed Erik as suffering from generalized anxiety disorder, the inability to control his restlessness, worry and irritability. Dietz had interviewed Erik for 16 hours at the Beverly Hills Police Department. The defense contended that Erik suffered from Post-Traumatic Stress Disorder. Dietz testified that it was impossible to diagnosis Erik with this disorder because he had no way of knowing if the events that were allegedly were true. Dietz also rejected other conclusions presented by the defense's expert witnesses. Dietz testified that Erik did not suffer from "learned helplessness," a symptom of Post-Traumatic Stress Disorder. Dietz pointed out that Erik bought two shotguns, loaded his weapon, and went to the shooting range to learn how to fire the weapon. This behavior showed rebelliousness and assertiveness inconsistent with the passiveness of learned helplessness.

Judge Weissberg did not allow Vicary to testify as he had in the first trial when he testified that he believed Erik's claims of molestation and that Erik killed his parents out of fear. Vicary was allowed to testify as a rebuttal witness regarding Erik's anxiety disorders. The result was that Vicary was a much less effective witness during the second trial.

On February 16, Judge Weissberg ruled that there was insufficient evidence that the brothers were in imminent danger when they fatally shot their parents on August 20, 1989 and that the "imperfect self-defense" jury instruction that the defense sought would not be read to the jury after closing arguments. The "imperfect self-defense" theory was at the center of the defense in the first trial and convinced some of the jurors on each of the two panels to vote to convict the brothers of manslaughter instead of murder.

Judge Weissberg ruled that the defense could argue that the brothers shot José in the heat of passion, but not Kitty. Weissberg ruled that there was sufficient evidence to show that José might have provoked his sons into committing a homicide, but there was insufficient evidence to show that Kitty provoked her sons.

On February 20, Conn began the first of four days of closing arguments. He ridiculed the brothers' claims of abuse as "the silliest, most ridiculous story ever told in a courtroom." Throughout his closing argument, Conn's tone was belittling and sarcastic. Conn urged the jurors to find the brothers guilty of first degree murder and not manslaughter. He attacked the testimony of Erik and said that it was self-serving and filled with lies and inconsistencies. Conn told jurors that they should reject Erik's claims that his father sexually abused him.

On February 26, Abramson began the first of three days of closing arguments. She accused David Conn of presenting fraudulent witnesses in an effort to win a case for "political reasons." Abramson was trying to point out to the jury that the Los Angeles County district attorney's office was under enormous pressure to win a "big case" after losing the McMartin preschool molestation cases, the first Menendez trial and the O.J. Simpson murder trial. She attacked Conn for using the taped confession from the December 11, 1989. Abramson attacked the prosecution theory that the brothers fired shots at José and Kitty's knees in order to make the killings appear to be a Mafia hit. She argued that the crime scene indicated that the killings were "highly emotional overkill" and not a professional hit.

Abramson told the jury that Erik had a mental disorder, Post-Traumatic Stress Disorder, and was in a state of mind at the time of the killings where he did not harbor malice. Abramson attacked the prosecution's theory that the brothers killed for money. "Parricide doesn't happen for money," she said. Abramson concluded her closing arguments with an emotional plea. She told the jury how close she had grown to Erik and that it would be "the ultimate tragedy" in her life if he were convicted.

Gessler's closing argument was low-key. He attacked the prosecution arguments that the brothers killed their parents in order to get their hands on their money. He said that Lyle believed he was disinherited and would lose his means of support if his parents died. Gessler asked the jurors to find Lyle not guilty of murdering Kitty and guilty only of manslaughter in the death of José. Gessler compared the Menendez case to a Greek tragedy, suggesting that José and Kitty had brought about their own demise because of fatal mortal flaws. Gessler added that José caused his own death by molesting his sons and making them believe that they could not escape from him. The brothers felt that their only option was to arm themselves. Gessler argued that Kitty brought about her own death by not protecting her sons and by making them believe that she was an enforcer of her husband's abuse.

On February 29, closing arguments ended with Conn telling the jury that Lyle and Erik blamed their victims, put their parents on trial, created a clever abuse excuse and told many lies in order to justify shooting their parents.

On March 1, the jury began to deliberate. On March 14, Judge Weissberg removed two female jurors, including the foreperson for medical reasons. The foreperson had suffered a heart attack and another female juror had gone into premature labor. One male alternative juror and one female alternative juror replaced the two female jurors. Jury deliberations would begin all over. This second jury consisted of eight men and four women.

On March 20, after four days of deliberation, the jury convicted the Menendez brothers each of two counts of first degree murder, as well as conspiracy to commit murder. Jurors also found that there were two special circumstances attached to the murders: lying in wait and multiple murder. Because special circumstances were found, there were only two sentencing options: life in prison without the possibility of parole or death by execution. The same jury that found the brothers guilty of first-degree murder would deliberate after a second, smaller trial, called the penalty phase, to determine the brothers' sentences.

Punishment

The penalty phase began on March 22, 1996 and was completed in three weeks. The defense called 18 witnesses to testify on behalf of the brothers. The rules of evidence were different in the penalty phase than at the brothers' trial. Since the jurors are being asked to make a life or death decision, the defense was permitted to appeal to the jury's sympathy. The rules allowed the defense to offer evidence of mitigating factors, such as the brothers' ages, whether they were "under the influence of extreme mental or emotional distress," whether the victims "were participants in their own deaths" and any other evidence that diminished the gravity of the crime.

On April 4, during the second week of the penalty phase, an unexpected and stunning thing happened in court. Dr. Vicary, the psychiatrist who had treated Erik since 1990, admitted that he doctored his notes at the direction of Leslie Abramson. Under cross-examination, Vicary admitted that he omitted from his notes entire sections containing incriminating statements by Erik Menendez. This incident had major ramifications for the defense.

On April 5, Abramson invoked her Fifth Amendment privilege not to incriminate herself when she refused to answer two questions about her possible misconduct regarding Vicary's notes.

After hearing arguments outside the presence of the jury, Judge Weissberg rejected defense motions for mistrials for both brothers. The defense had tried to argue that a mistrial should be declared because of Abramson's ineffective assistance of counsel. Weissberg ruled that Lyle could not make that argument because Abramson was not his lawyer. Weissberg also ruled that Barry Levine was perfectly capable of taking over Erik's case, if Abramson decided not to continue to participate in the proceedings.

On April 6, Conn told the court how he learned about the deleted notes. Conn said that in 1993 Abramson had turned over to him the redacted version of Vicary's notes. At some point during the trial, Conn needed to review the notes at the Van Nuys courthouse, but had left his copy in his office in downtown Los Angeles. Conn borrowed a copy of the notes from Dr. Dietz who had received a copy from the defense. Somehow, Dietz had been given a copy of the original notes. Conn said that Abramson turned over the originals by accident and had if it not been for this mistake, no one would have noticed the discrepancy. Vicary had deleted 24 pages of statements Erik had made to him and rewrote 10 pages of notes.

The notes contained incriminating evidence against Erik. One of the sections noted that Erik told Vicary that he thought about what it would be like to live without his parents. In another section, Erik told Vicary that he and Lyle discussed doing something "drastic" but the notes do not specify exactly what is meant by "drastic." In another section, Erik told Vicary that José's homosexual lover visited the mansion two days before the murders occurred and told the brothers that their parents were going to kill them. Vicary later admitted that Erik told him that this story was a lie.

On April 9, Judge Weissberg ruled that a conflict did not exist between Leslie Abramson and Erik Menendez that would necessitate her removal from the trial. The ruling followed two days of closed-door hearings during which Gessler and Levine sought to have Abramson removed. It was only after Erik Menendez spoke to Weissberg behind closed doors that Abramson was allowed to stay. Weissberg said that he would instruct the jury not to consider Abramson's alleged actions of misconduct when deciding whether the brothers should be sentenced to death or life in prison. Weissberg also ruled that the prosecution could not ask Vicary about Abramson's order to delete his notes, instead Weissberg directed the prosecutors to impeach Vicary's testimony without making any references to Abramson. Leslie Abramson remained silent throughout the remainder of the trial.

On April 10, Vicary concluded his testimony and the prosecution presented three rebuttal witnesses: Les Zoeller and Kitty's two brothers, Milton and Brian Andersen.

On April 11, David Conn gave his closing argument. Conn argued that the Menendez brothers should be sentenced to death because they chose to kill their parents in a "horrifying and brutal way." Conn ridiculed the defense allegations of psychological abuse, saying that the allegations were "desperate and trivial."

In his closing argument, Barry Levine accused the Los Angeles County district attorney's office of arbitrarily deciding who was eligible for the death penalty. He reminded the jury of the O.J. Simpson case and said, "he's not even eligible for the death penalty." Levine told the jury that the prosecution had not presented evidence of aggravating circumstances other that the crime itself.

On April 12, the jury began to deliberate whether the Menendez brothers should be sentenced to life in prison or death.

On April 17, 1996, after deliberating for three days, the jury decided that life in prison was the appropriate punishment for Lyle and Erik Menendez. The jury later said that the abuse defense was never a factor in their deliberations and that the jury decided to spare the brothers' lives because neither brother had a felony record or a history of violence. Although some jurors said they were sympathetic to the brothers' upbringing and that it may have contributed to the murders being committed, in the end they could not excuse it. Several of the jurors believed some of the evidence of psychological abuse, but questioned whether the sexual abuse occurred.

Unlike the first trial where two separate juries could not agree on whether the brothers committed murder or manslaughter, jurors in the retrial said that there was never any division or dissent and there were no holdouts. None of the jurors

167

believed the defense theory that the brothers killed because they were afraid and the jurors did not believe that the brothers killed solely to get their hands on their parents' money.

On June 1, defense attorneys for the Menendez brothers filed a motion in Judge Weissberg's court seeking a new trial for the brothers. The motion argued that Judge Weissberg erred when he refused to allow the jury to consider manslaughter verdicts. The motion also claimed that Judge Weissberg erred when he allowed jurors to hear the December 11, 1989 tape of the brothers confessing to Dr. Oziel. The motion also claimed that Weissberg erred when he limited the number of defense witnesses who testified about the Menendezes' family life.

Lyle and Erik

Prior to being formally sentenced on July 2, 1996, Lyle and Erik gave an interview to Barbara Walters for the television program 20/20. The purpose of the interview was to gain public support for the brothers' bid to be imprisoned together. A committee of California state correction officials ultimately made the decision of whether to imprison the brothers together. David Conn said that he had no position on whether the brothers were imprisoned together or apart, as long as they did not receive any special treatment.

On July 2, 1996, Judge Weissberg sentenced Lyle and Erik Menendez to life in prison without the possibility of parole. Judge Weissberg sentenced the brothers to consecutive sentences for the murders and the charge of conspiracy to commit murder.

A few weeks after the sentences were announced, Lyle and Erik were taken to the North Kern State Prison at Delano, a Department of Corrections reception center outside of Los Angeles for diagnostic evaluation. A decision whether the brothers were to be imprisoned together was made after the evaluation was completed.

The Aftermath

Two television films were made about the Menendez murders, between their first and second trials. The first was 'Honour Thy Father and Mother: The True Story of the Menendez Murders' (1994), starring James Farentino (José), Jill Clayburgh (Kitty), Billy Warlock (Lyle), and David Beron (Erik). The second was 'Menendez: A Killing in Beverly Hills' (1994), starring Edward James Olmos (José), Beverly D'Angelo (Kitty), Damian Chapa (Lyle), and Travis Fine (Erik).

The film 'The Cable Guy' (1996) parodied the Menendez trials and had Ben Stiller playing both brothers. There is a reference to Lyle Menendez in the film 'Jane Austen's Mafia!' (1998). The play 'Lion Hunting in North America', by playwright Jonah Maidoff, is based on the Menendez murders.

The Menendez brothers are currently in prisons in California, Lyle is in Mule Creek State Prison whilst Erik is in the Pleasant Valley State Prison. Both brothers have married whilst in prison but are denied conjugal rights.

Erik's wife, Tammi Menendez, published a book 'They Said We'd Never Make It – My Life with Erik Menendez' (2005). Subsequent to the book's publishing, Erik appeared on the Larry King Live show and confirmed that he had made a large contribution to the editing of Tammi's book.

He also said that he and Lyle had not spoken in more than 10 years. The brothers are expected to spend the remainder of their natural lives in prison, and to both die without ever consummating their marriages.

In Closing

On August 2, 1996, Dr. William Vicary was removed from the panel of mental health professionals appointed by Los Angeles Superior County judges to analyze and testify about defendants in court cases. A ten-member committee made up of Superior Court judges reviewed the transcripts of the Menendez brothers' retrial and decided that Vicary's "continued participation on the panel was inappropriate." Later, the California State Medical Board sued Vicary in an attempt to revoke his license. Vicary was able to reach an agreement with the Medical Board to retain his license after admitting that he acted unethically during the Menendez case.

On September 10, 1996, the California Department of Corrections separated the Menendez brothers. Lyle was bussed from the North Kern State Prison to the California Correctional Institution near Tehachapi and Erik was bussed to the California State Prison, near Sacramento. Lyle and Erik were segregated from other prisoners and classified as maximum-security inmates.

Leslie Abramson was critical of the Department of Corrections decision to separate the brothers and said that the move was "unduly cruel and punitive." On the other hand, Les Zoeller said that he was "pleased the brothers finally are apart." Zoeller added, "I think that by putting them together, everybody's at risk."

On January 26, 1997, David Conn was notified that he would be transferred to the Norwalk office of the district attorney's office. After the Menendez verdicts, Conn gave an interview to the *Los Angeles Times* were he stated that he "wouldn't mind one day being the Los Angeles district attorney." Conn was later passed over for promotion and removed as acting head deputy of the major crimes unit. Conn said he was humiliated that he was not promoted and he backed an opponent of Gil Garcetti's in the November 1996 Los Angeles district attorney's race.

On October 13, 1997, after an 11-month investigation, Leslie Abramson learned that she would not be prosecuted by the Los Angeles district attorney's office for requesting that Dr. Vicary delete sections of his notes during the retrial of the brothers.

In 1997, Dr. Oziel surrendered his psychotherapist's license and moved from California to another state.

On February 27, 1998, the California Court of Appeals upheld the murder convictions of Lyle and Erik Menendez. The court's opinion established no new precedents and found that Judge Weissberg made no errors in a series of controversial rulings that limited the defense testimony about the brothers' upbringing and mental states during the retrial. The opinion was not published in official law reports and indicated that the justices on the Court of Appeals did not intend to create any legal precedents that could apply to future cases.

On May 28, 1998, the California Supreme Court voted to uphold the murder convictions and life-without-parole sentences of Lyle and Erik Menendez. None of the Supreme Court justices voted to review the case. Lyle's appellate lawyer, Cliff Gardner, said that he planned to file an appeal in federal court.

In 1998, David Conn left the district attorney's office for private practice.

On February 9, 1999, the State Bar of California closed its three year investigation of Leslie Abramson after deciding that there was insufficient evidence to conclude she violated ethical rules in the Menendez brothers retrial.

Leslie Abramson continues to practice criminal law in Los Angeles. She recently defended Jeremy Strohmeyer, the teenager who killed a young girl in a Nevada casino. She also appears as a court commentator on ABC's Nightline and on Court TV.

A new California law was passed which states that if the abuse the defendant suffered was not allowed to be mentioned in their trial, they could file an appeal. For the Menendez brothers, this was the break they had been waiting nearly three decades for. They felt certain that if the judge allowed them to bring up the alleged abuse in the second trial, they wouldn't have been found guilty of first-degree murder. At the moment, the Menendez brothers do not have a new court date. They are hoping to file an appeal and appear in court before 2020, the deadline to file the appeal under the new law.

If the brothers would go to trial today, would they be able to convince another jury or even an appeal judge that they shouldn't spend the rest of their lives in prison?

Made in the USA
Columbia, SC
26 October 2017